HOMOSEXUALITY:
A Biblical View

HOMOSEXUALITY:
A Biblical View

Greg L. Bahnsen

BAKER BOOK HOUSE
Grand Rapids, Michigan 49506

Unless otherwise indicated Scripture quotations are the author's own translation.

References marked NIV are from the New International Version, New Testament, © 1973 by New York Bible Society International, © 1974 by New York International Bible Society. Used by permission.

References marked NASB are from the New American Standard Bible, © The Lockman Foundation, 1960, 1962, 1963, 1968, 1971, 1972, 1973. Used by permission.

Contents

Preface

Historically Christians have taught that people do not have an unlimited right to do with their bodies as they please. Such a view is undermined today by defenders of three discernible and outspoken factions in our culture: feminists, abortionists, and homosexuals. Ethical questions pertaining to this last group are examined in the present study. While specific variations within sexual identity and orientation are recognized, the general term *homosexual* will be used here for any person, male or female (thus including lesbians), who engages in sexual relations with members of the same sex or who desires to do so. Homosexuality is an affectional attraction to or active sexual relation with a person of the same sex.

The ironic problem with the modern discussion of homosexuality is its virtually uncritical perpetuation of cultural prejudices—despite its espoused openmindedness and neutralized bias. Certain questionable assumptions in ethics, the human sciences, and political thought have misled our society toward tolerance for homosexuality in personal, ecclesiastical, and civil spheres. Study of the Scriptures should bring one to contest those popular assumptions and has convinced me that homosexuality ought to be challenged in all three of these areas. Individuals should disapprove of and oppose homosexuality as immoral. Churches should decline membership and office to unrepentant homosexuals. States should restrain homosexuality rather than making it a civil right. We must equally insist that individuals not take a holier-than-thou attitude toward homosexual sin, that churches faithfully proclaim the good news of deliverance to homosexuals, and that the state not persecute them by entrapment, invasion of privacy, or intentionally selective and uneven attention.

The grounds for these conclusions are explained in the following pages. My aim has been to investigate various aspects of the moral question about homosexuality, attempting to be faithful to the full Word of God in its own multiple facets: law and gospel, restraint and rehabilitation, individual and society, church and state, etc. Throughout I have attempted, in a teachable attitude, to think God's thoughts after Him. Readers and critics will hopefully measure my success by the standard of God's objective and reliable written Word.

Before proceeding to the study itself, however, a few words are called for in answer to the "rhetorical terrorism" (as one writer puts it)[1] of certain polemicists for homosexuality and alleged homosexual rights.[2] Pontification, accusation, name-calling, attribution of evil motives to opponents, etc., often contribute to fallacious reasoning and serve to browbeat the gullible into agreement with defenders of homosexuality. For instance, contrary to a common retort, disagreeing with homosexuals about their rights and disapproving of their behavior does not automati-

---

[1]M. J. Sobran, "Bogus Sex," *Human Life Review*, Vol. III, No. 4 (Fall, 1977).

[2]I do not mean to suggest that only defenders of homosexuals are guilty of this. With Christian embarrassment we confess that opponents of homosexuality have not completely abstained from the same kind of tactic. Not all readers may think that I have either, but it has been my intention.

cally make someone a bigot. His opposition is not necessarily a violent hatred or exaggerated fear, rooted in unfair and irrational attitudes based on blanket preconceptions; it is not an infallible evidence of "homophobia." Opposition to homosexuality need not be motivated by a prejudiced and insulting attitude toward a group of people as such. A fair and dispassionate examination of the evidence relevant to an ethical evaluation of homosexual acts and affections can very well support a negative moral conclusion held with principled conviction. Viewing something as immoral is not the same thing as being bigoted; for example, it is not customary to look on someone who condemns the killing of innocent people as a bigot toward murderers. (If it were customary, we would then have to distinguish between honorable and dishonorable bigotry.)

Another frequent polemic maintains that those who criticize homosexuality are guilty of having a judgmental attitude. It has been said that "surely it is neither the Christian's responsibility nor prerogative to judge other people's life-styles." One self-professed "evangelical" study of homosexuality goes so far as to accuse its opponents of false witness and blasphemy against the Holy Spirit! If meant to be taken seriously, these are misguided remarks. To be true to God and His Word we cannot be uncritical of or neutral toward those things Scripture prohibits. People must be warned against attitudes and behavior that are displeasing to a holy God. Those who have been redeemed by the mercy of God are called to conscious separation from sin and emulation of God's character; these would be impossible without identifying some things as sinful and ungodly—which is patently judgmental. The fact is that Scripture does not forbid judging in itself, but judging which is ill-motivated, hasty, unfair, or according to unbiblical standards. Indeed, God in His Word requires us to judge actions[3] and to reprove the unfruitful works of

---

[3]Matt. 7:15–23; cf. John 7:24.

darkness[4]—but without partiality,[5] hypocrisy,[6] or attempting to determine inward matters pertaining to an individual's heart.[7] It is the spirit of this age that demands the general suppression of discernment, encourages unprincipled tolerance, and criticizes anyone who would dare to criticize. The Holy Spirit exhorts us to "prove all things; hold fast that which is good; abstain from every form of evil."[8]

Another rhetorical taunt commonly cast at opponents of homosexuality today is that they are stern and legalistic, lack love, and ignore the realm of personal concerns in ethics. However, this accusation rests on faulty assumptions. First, legalism means using the law as a way of self-salvation, not the heart-felt desire of the redeemed to obey the commands of their Lord and Savior.[9] Second, concern for God's blessed law is not deficient in love but identified with it.[10] Third, person-centered concerns are not antagonistic to unchanging moral norms; the perfect Son of God, who was dedicated to obeying God's law completely,[11] is the model of genuine personality and morality, and we are to be conformed to His likeness.[12] Those who promote unbiblical norms in ethics in the name of "authentic personality" are in reality being anti-personal; the norms of Scripture are abrasive only to those who fail to have a living, saving, personal relationship with God through Christ. Ironically, such critics usually propose to *set aside* explicit biblical teaching and substitute for it modern values, so as to *retain* the "scriptural" concern for personal value![13] The obvious result of this line of

---

[4]Eph. 5:11; 1 Tim. 5:20; 2 Tim. 4:2; Titus 1:13; 2:15.
[5]1 Tim. 5:21.
[6]Matt. 7:1–5.
[7]1 Sam. 16:7.
[8]1 Thess. 5:21, 22; cf. 1 John 4:1.
[9]Ezek. 11:19, 20; Rom. 8:1–4; 2 Cor. 5:14, 15; Rom. 6:1—7:6; Titus 2:11–14; Rom. 3:31.
[10]Rom. 13:8–10; 1 John 5:2, 3; 2 John 6; John 14:15,21,23; 15:9,10.
[11]John 15:10; Heb. 7:26–28; Ps. 40:7,8; cf. Heb. 10:4–10.
[12]Col. 3:10; Eph. 4:13,24; 2 Cor. 3:18; 4:4; 1 John 2:5,6.
[13]Carl F. H. Henry, "In and Out of the Gay World," *Is Gay Good?*, ed. W. Dwight Oberholtzer (Philadelphia: Westminster Press, 1971), pp. 105,106.

thinking is the attitude that explicit biblical teaching is often "reprehensible," "repugnant," and "irrelevant,"[14] that enlightened modern men must take a "discriminating" approach to what the Bible teaches,[15] and that those who do not are guilty of "bibliolatry."[16] The choice before us thus seems to be this: either we will discriminate against homosexuals, or we will discriminate against the Word of God. We will either aim to convert the homosexual and have him transformed into the image of Christ, or we will aim to convert the church's thinking about God's Word and transform the Christian ethic into the image of homosexual values. The discussion has brought us to the question of ultimate priorities and standards, and here the choice for the Christian ought not be difficult.[17]

In conclusion, opposition to homosexuality is not a sure sign of a bigoted, improperly judgmental, or legalistic attitude. It is rhetorical terrorism to charge otherwise. Such fallacious tactics may persuade the unwary, but they cannot annul or disprove convictions rooted in the revealed Word of God. Our responsibility, of course, is to be sure that our attitudes do accord with Scripture and are not simply reflecting past tradition or mimicking present prejudice.

Whether the incidence and prevalence of homosexuality are actually higher in our day or not, I am not sure. However, there can be little doubt that the *visibility* of homosexuality is much higher. The organized and unorganized movement to dignify homosexuality and gain tolerance for it has infiltrated every sector of society and every area of culture: from the church to the television, from education to legislation. This is not a time for Christians to be silent or despairing, oblivious and inactive. As

---

[14]Thomas Maurer, "Toward a Theology of Homosexuality—Tried and Found Trite and Tragic," *Is Gay Good?*, pp. 98–100.
[15]Lewis Williams, "Walls of Ice—Theology and Social Policy," *Is Gay Good?*, pp. 168, 169.
[16]Joseph Fletcher, "Preface," *Is Gay Good?*, p. 8.
[17]Col. 1:18; 2 Cor. 10:5; Job 40:2; 1 Kings 22:14; Isa, 8:20; 2 Tim. 3:16,17; Rom. 3:4; 9:20; 1 Cor. 14:37,38; 2 Thess. 3:14; 1 John 4:6; Matt. 7:24–27; John 12:48; Matt. 5:19.

Jesus' parable says, "while men slept, the enemy came and sowed tares."[18] It is time to awaken and to let the light of the world shine through us, scattering the sinful darkness.[19] And to do this requires that we properly understand the message of God. To that end I hope this book will be beneficial to Christ's church.

Carl F. H. Henry is right when he says, "The people of God will of course want to see a society in which the commandments of God hold full sway."[20] In this book I argue, with a view to the present controversy in our country, that homosexuality is not to be viewed as a civil right. However, we would not only recognize the purpose of God through civil government to coercively restrain crime and disorder, but also confess that gospel-believing churches have the spiritual resources that alone can redeem and change the hearts of offenders so that they desire to live righteous lives. A deep-felt concern for the proper attitudes of Christ's people, the power of the gospel, the justice of the state, and the ultimate well-being of the homosexual has prompted the following study.

In writing up the results of my research and reflection, I have purposely avoided the scholarly apparatus of extensively footnoting the sources of opinions which are criticized. I have done so, first, because there is a wealth of diverse expression, yet only a basic number of exegetically and ethically relevant arguments; second, because this has made it possible to organize, synthesize, and in some places strengthen the polemic for homosexuality which Christians need to answer; and, third, to render the text easier to follow for a wider scope of readers. Those interested in bibliographic background are referred to the extensive list of books and articles for further research at the end of this book. Although the bibliography of books is detailed into various categories, it has been possible to provide a thorough list of

---

[18]Matt. 13:25.
[19]Eph. 5:14, cf. vv. 6–13; Matt. 5:14–16; John 8:12; 1 John 1:5–7; John 1:5.
[20]Henry, "In and Out of the Gay World," *Is Gay Good*, pp. 105, 106.

periodical articles for the most part only in the generally religious field. Helpful lists of periodical articles of a medical, psychological, sociological, and historical nature can be found in Arno Karlen's *Sexuality and Homosexuality: A New View* (New York: W. W. Norton & Co., 1971) and W. D. Oberholtzer's *Is Gay Good?* (Philadelphia: Westminster Press, 1971).

In preparing this study for publication I have received the indispensable help of others. First and foremost I wish to express my gratitude to Jane and Dennis Johnson for their stylistic and editorial improvement of the text, making it much more readable and clear. Previously they had gained experience in reworking my pieces for our college newspaper, and it has been to my matchless benefit here to have their collaboration again. I am indebted to such friends. I also want to thank certain members of my presbytery who criticized earlier versions of this manuscript; even where we may still differ, I have profited from comments they have made. I would also express appreciation to Dr. Ronald Enroth, author of *The Gay Church*, for his course in the sociology of deviant behavior, which a few years ago forced me to start thinking through the issues explored in this book. Finally, I am thankful to Mrs. Elaine Connell and Mr. David Gillespie for their painstaking work in getting the manuscript ready for publication; Elaine twice labored long in typing it, and David has been of great help in proofreading, filling out the bibliographies, and preparing the index. Although all of these people deserve commendation, naturally I am alone responsible for whatever defects are contained in the book.

And speaking of defects, let me acknowledge right here that the present study does not come close to saying everything that could and should be said in the areas of moral theology, exegesis of biblical passages touching on homosexuality, scientific studies of alleged homosexual propensity and etiology, the response of the church, how homosexuals should be counseled, or the principles of civil legislation and social discrimination. I have not tried to speak the last word on these subjects, a choice which many will immediately recognize as judicious! I do hope that what is rehearsed in the following pages will be of service to sincere Christians attempting to make their way through the confusing maze of current opinion. But I disclaim having said anything definitive on the subject. I am sure that my critics will not be tempted to think otherwise. Of them I only request a fair hearing and a charitable discussion of the principle and inferences that have formed the conclusions of this book.

As I finish this preface a news release has come to my attention, saying that a mainline Presbyterian denomination has received a report from the task force it appointed to study homosexuality, recommending that the General Assembly not view homosexuality in itself as a sin which precludes ordination and that homosexual acts between consenting adults be decriminalized in society. This only testifies further to the confusion that has overcome our day. Again we can see the urgency of the church becoming mindful of its biblical roots and attaining a clear, Christ-honoring mindset with respect to homosexuality as a sin and a crime. Today the clarity of God's Word must be proclaimed without wavering, lest we fail in the Great Commission given us by our Lord.

Reformed Theological Seminary   Greg L. Bahnsen
Jackson, Mississippi   January 23, 1978

1

Basic Commitments

The church of Jesus Christ is being called upon repeatedly, both from within and without, to reappraise its historic posture toward homosexuality. Once the church proclaimed the necessity of repenting of homosexuality as sinful and endorsed its prohibition by civil authorities. Now it is told that new approaches in biblical studies and newly discovered data in psychology and sociology should lead it to abandon such an impractical pastoral approach and to renounce such an unjust social policy. The overworked vocabulary of liberation and tolerance is pressed into service, as are charges of unfounded fear and prejudicial stereotyping. It is thought that the present enlightened and compassionate atmosphere of study should foster a healthy view of sex in which all civil restraints against homosexuality would be erased and the form of one's sexual gratification would be considered morally indifferent.

Such a prevailing public challenge demands a response from those charged with shepherding the flock of God, teaching the disciples of Christ, and refuting those who oppose His truth. In the spirit of the Reformers, they must labor so that God's truth is not obscured by the traditions of men. Against the drift of society

and the delusions of the natural man the church must present a
prophetic witness, calling men to repentance and teaching the
nations to observe whatever the Lord has commanded. It is scan-
dalous to suggest that one can enter the kingdom or promote its
ends in society while rebelling against the standards of the King.
For these reasons the present study has been prepared in the
twofold conviction that the church must urge men by the mercies
of God to be transformed through the renewing of their minds
rather than being conformed to the world,[1] and that the state and
its rulers must act as servants of God, avenging His displeasure
against evildoers.[2]

The Foundational Question of Scripture

Differing attitudes toward homosexuality within the professing
Christian church can often be traced to conflicting views of Scripture. Many disputes over the morality of homosexuality turn on
another question: will Scripture be the Christian's normative
guide or must it yield that position of authority over ethics to
modern scholarship, personal experience, natural reason, new
mystical insights, public opinion, or some other standard? The
twentieth century has proved to be an age of increasing doctrinal
permissiveness among professing Christian teachers; this trend
emerged from the modernist abandonment of the absolute authority of God's revealed Word in the Old and New Testaments.
Contrary to Scripture's own self-witness as God's inspired and
infallible Word, many churchmen have attempted to synthesize
Christian commitment with humanistic or secular perspectives in
philosophy and the sciences. Throughout the theological spectrum the effect has been distortions of the Christian message that
are evident to any thoughtful student.

---

[1]Rom. 12:2.
[2]Rom. 13:4.

Moreover, the alarming aftermath of replacing the God-centered theology of the Bible with the man-centered outlook of worldly wisdom is the amazing capacity of many churchmen to tolerate any and every deviation from the clearcut biblical standards of morality. By suppressing the truth in unrighteousness they can make concessions to homosexuality, granting it either sympathy or hearty approval. In Romans 1:18–32 Paul depicts this progression—from exchanging God's truth for a lie to approving unnatural sexual inversion—as the object of divine displeasure.

Paul's teaching has received startling confirmation in the enlightened atmosphere of modern theological study, where perversion of the truth about God has produced a corresponding perversion regarding man, God's image. In an idolatrous fashion man has become the focus and authority of unorthodox theology, with the result that he has been debased through homosexual self-love at the very point of the essential distinction between male and female. Departure from the Word of God to other "lords" over life is theological inversion, a denial of the distinction between the Creator and His creation. Theological inversion today advertises its disgraceful, ungodly character by fostering sexual inversion in man as God's image, denying the male/female distinction in creation.

The justification of this disordered sexual orientation in contemporary theological literature, grounded in a refusal to be directed by God's Word, demonstrates dramatically that the self-professed wisdom of many theologians' secular mindset is, in fact, foolishness with God. It is time to recognize the depths of sin to which the liberal and humanistic attitude toward Scripture is prone. When revealed theology is reduced to an autonomous study of man, when biblical authority is replaced by an unstable human wisdom, when behavior is directed by the descriptions of social science instead of the prescriptions of God's Word, then we have returned to the situation prevailing at the time of the Book of Judges: every man will do what is right in his own eyes.

As the church takes a fresh look at the moral question of homosexuality, therefore, it must recognize that without God's clear, infallible Word and its pronouncements Christianity has nothing to contribute to the issue. Without an authoritative word from the Lord regarding homosexuality there is no distinctive Christian discipleship in reference to it, nor is there a Christian word of hope for the individual or society. If theologians are not heralds of the King's Word, proclaimers of divine revelation, then their pronouncements are just more opinions among many others, and they deserve no special hearing. Christian standards are defined by the revealed Word of God in Scripture. Men can accept God's prescriptive will for behavior or they can reject it, but they cannot tamper with it. If the biblical witness offends them, then it is God whom they must blame and reproach.

The church cannot condone what God condemns in Scripture without losing its own integrity and coming under His judgment. For the true disciple of Christ, moral boundaries are never drawn by man but only and always by God. Therefore, it should be noticed at the outset of this study that many cases arguing for tolerance of homosexuality are based on doctrinal premises that deviate from biblical teaching. Those who put forth such arguments cannot be seen as attempting to worship the living and true God as He directs and desires. Their antipathy to biblical revelation means that they will follow something less than the God of the Bible, who is the only Lord recognized by the believer.

There is a sense, therefore, in which recent requests for the church to review its attitude toward homosexuality are really a challenge to the church's very identity, purpose, and direction and a challenge to its view of the Word of God. Such calls for reappraisal require a defense of the authority of the Bible—a defense that is, and has been, readily available elsewhere. It is assumed here that the authority of the Bible, for which it ought to be believed and obeyed, depends not on popular endorsement and human wisdom but completely upon its divine Author and

His self-attesting identification of Scripture as the Word of God. While the philosophical argument and external evidences for the Bible's truth are objective and inescapable, our full persuasion of the divine authority of Scripture comes as the Holy Spirit bears witness by and with the self-attesting Word in our hearts. Proponents of homosexuality who are indifferent to the authority of God's Word and its teaching about this practice will obviously require such a basic defense of biblical authority.

Yet the defense of the faith at the foundational level of Scripture's authority is only preliminary, for much of the modern challenge to the church's condemnation of homosexuality is not grounded openly in a repudiation of the Bible's teaching. Professing Christian advocates of moral tolerance toward homosexuality have recently alleged that a correct reading of the biblical record will undermine the belief that it condemns all homosexual activity, independent of circumstances. They claim that there is no clear revelation of God's will that prohibits homosexuality as we understand that condition today. Moreover, they believe that scriptural ethics focus on personal considerations and situational factors, while condemning preoccupation with rigid legal stipulations.

Finally, even if it could be shown that God's law should form the Christian ethic and that homosexuality as such is to be condemned, it is still maintained that this is a private matter of personal morality—not something that the state should recognize and prohibit in society at large. That is, even if homosexuality is a sin, it should not be deemed a crime by the state, according to some Christian writers; for them sexual preference is a civil right, a matter indifferent to public morality in a pluralistic society. Consequently, the basic defense of biblical authority must be supplemented today with answers for recent challenges to the traditional interpretation and application of Scripture regarding sexual inversion. The remainder of this study is given over to this task.

How should the Christian understand and morally evaluate homosexuality? Some church teachers reject its acceptability and would apply ecclesiastical and civil sanctions against it; others would omit the latter. Some teachers reject the acceptability of homosexuality; however, they would not apply any discriminatory or punitive sanctions to it in either ecclesiastical or civil life. Others would take a mediating or qualified position, accepting homosexuality under some conditions. Still others would grant homosexuality full acceptance and view its practice as morally neutral. The particular attitude assumed by the disciple of Christ must be determined by the Word of God: "If anyone loves me, he will keep my word."[3]

The supreme judge by which all religious controversies are to be determined and all human opinions are to be examined can be no other than the Holy Spirit speaking in the Scripture. For that reason it is necessary to study particular passages of the Bible that speak of homosexuality. But first a word is required about the broad hermeneutical assumptions and procedures that will be involved in this study. Too often, interpreters employ excessive ingenuity and exegetical gymnastics to reconcile biblical teaching with what they want to believe. However, if we can reinterpret Scripture to endorse homosexuality, then we can make it endorse anything else anyone would like to do or believe. Consequently, a preliminary word about interpretation is appropriate.

By saving faith a Christian believes whatever is revealed in the Word of God to be true, and he responds to the biblical commands by yielding due obedience to them and by trembling at their threats. The believer approaches the Bible as fully authoritative—inerrant in its assertions, binding in its requirements. Accordingly, he views the biblical teaching as unified and consistent, without pitting one portion or author against another, but rather acknowledging "the consent of all the parts and entire

---

[3]John 14:23.

perfection thereof." In understanding individual texts, moreover, the Christian will take into account their local contexts and their specific literary genres. Furthermore, the individual text, interpreted in its local context, will also be read in the light of the Bible as a whole, preventing contradiction and keeping in focus the centrality of Christ and His redemptive economy.

It follows from these considerations that the infallible rule of interpretation of Scripture is the Scripture itself. The evidence of the biblical text itself must have priority in its interpretation over the results of other scholarly disciplines. Since our study of creation through the sciences must presuppose biblical truth, the results and explanations of disciplines dealing with general revelation must be weighed in terms of God's special revelation. This fact does not mean that cultural history should not be studied to understand the biblical writers better; such background considerations are, in fact, necessary to insure that our present cultural situation and modern perceptions of religion are not foisted upon the scriptural material, deforming its doctrine. Finally, in all theological controversies ultimate appeal must be made to the original languages of Scripture, being immediately inspired by God and providentially preserved in all ages. This is required so that doctrinal conclusions may not be misled by faulty translations but conformed to the original meaning of God's revealed Word.

The Law as an Expression of God's Will

Before examining the biblical texts pertaining to homosexuality, it is necessary to discuss not only interpretation but also the general moral theology presented in God's Word. This need arises because of contemporary theology's hostility toward a normative approach to Christian ethics guided by unqualified divine commandments. Today ethicists shun any decision-making process which rests on an examination of God's law, maintaining that Scripture abhors such legalism and favors a situational or existential approach to morality.

Two things must be observed in response. First, the Bible certainly does lay stress on the goal of Christian ethics and the moral agent. The situations in which we attempt to live righteous lives, the consequences of our behavior, and the motivation and character of the righteous man are all of concern in the scriptural revelation of God's will for our lives.

But second, it must be remembered that such moral considerations are revealed by the Author of the law, and that they are presented along with divine commandments. The situational and personal factors in Christian ethics do not contradict absolute norms of morality set down in God's law. Indeed, when we look fully at our situation, we will bear in mind such factors as creation (man was made by God as morally responsible to His Word), the fall (natural conditions are not what they ought to be), redemption (sin no longer has dominion over the believer), and the ever-present special revelation of God (i.e., part of our situation is that revealed law which we either obey or disobey). When we consider that the goal of Christian living is to glorify God in all things and to seek first His kingdom, we realize our need for divine direction. When we consider the consequences of our actions, we cannot forget the final judgment, which will be according to the criteria of God's revealed Word. Therefore, a situational ethic demands that the Christian pay attention to God's law, which was given for man's good.[4] The same holds true for an existential ethic which is concerned with the character of the moral agent. God's law makes us new persons;[5] it is the pattern of ethical freedom[6] and the specific form of Christian

---

[4]Deut. 10:13.
[5]Ps. 19:7–14.
[6]Ps. 119:45; James 2:12.

love.[7] The internal work of the Spirit in the believer produces conformity to the law of God.[8]

Therefore, it is not contrary to biblical ethics or Christian morality to look to Scripture for divine commandments that bind us, without qualification, to a particular kind of behavior. The normative perspective of God's law cannot be suppressed in considering the way God wants man to live. Much of modern Christian ethics fails to understand that our situation is structured by redemptive history and includes a clear directive from God. It fails to understand that love is not without content or form but is defined by God's law. It fails to understand that the law is the pattern of sanctification and life for the believer—that by it he can pursue God's glory and kingdom, achieve the good God intends for man, and walk freely, lovingly, and spiritually. The righteous man can declare, "O how love I thy law! it is my meditation all the day."[9]

Of course "the wicked" walk in different counsels and scoff.[10] Biblical morality is an offense to the modern relativistic and hedonistic mentality. Those who view the homosexual as an innocent victim of harsh discrimination by the church and society deem God's revealed will as anachronistic and perverted. This response is ultimately unavoidable. Two opposing ethical systems will always condemn each other as a perversion. The mind set on the sinful nature of man is hostile to God and is unable to subject itself to His law;[11] yet he who delights in God's law burns with indignation toward the wicked who forsake it.[12] Divergent attitudes toward homosexuality are to be traced to different moral standards, different laws.

For the believer, the disciple of Christ, the servant of God,

---

[7]John 14:15; 1 John 5:3.
[8]Rom. 8:4.
[9]Ps. 119:97; cf. 1:2.
[10]Ps. 1:1.
[11]Rom. 8:5–8.
[12]Ps. 119:53.

every biblically condemned action or attitude is a transgression of the righteous law of God and, as such, brings man under His wrath, resulting in spiritual, temporal, and eternal miseries. Any deviation from God's holy will, no matter how small, deserves damnation. Therefore, the law of God and its precise details must be regarded with due respect by the Christian, despite the detractions and ridicule of those who cannot bear it as a standard of behavior. One must relinquish the impossible desire to please all men and finally settle on his ultimate moral commitment. The choice of differing standards will unavoidably generate enmity, but the follower of Christ is willing to bear the opposition it entails. He knows that the wicked will not stand in the judgment, and that their way will perish;[13] thus he purposes to take God's law as his moral authority and final criterion of righteousness, *whatever* that law may turn out to require. "Let God be found true, though every man is a liar!"[14]

Not only is God's law a necessary part of Christian ethics and an unquestionable standard of righteousness, it is a *relevant* guide for morality. Some writers propose that Christian morality needs to be updated—that a valid ethic cannot be established with respect to homosexuality today unless one takes into account modern data and scientific research and correlates the Christian attitude to them. Such a procedure indiscriminately accepts the "scientific" conclusions of modern psychology and sociology, despite their speculative presuppositions and faulty methods, and overlooks the fact that modern psychologists and sociologists are actually strongly divided in their theories and conclusions about homosexuality. More importantly, the attempt to generate a valid Christian ethic out of modern scientific research tends to commit the "naturalistic fallacy"—assuming that what is is what ought to be. What *is* the case often is not what *ought* to be the case, and

---

[13]Ps. 1:4–6.
[14]Rom. 3:4; cf. Job 40:2; Rom. 9:20.

for that reason a fallen perspective of the world cannot lead to binding and relevant standards of ethical obligation.

Christian ethics does not have its source in human research, evaluations, plans, or authority, but rather in the revealed Word of God. In His sight all things are open and manifest. His knowledge is infinite, infallible, and independent of the creature, and He is most holy in all His counsels, works, and commands. Because God is omniscient, because He has created man with his specific nature, because He sovereignly governs every event of history, God does not depend upon man's modern research to make His law applicable or relevant to man's every historical situation. Being the eternal creator and sustainer of the world and unchanging in His nature, God is not threatened with obsolescence; He and His law are relevant to every moment of finite man's existence.

Accordingly, the ancient Word of God will be the very standard of judgment on the final consummation day: "He who rejects me and does not receive my sayings has one who judges him; the word I spoke is what will judge him at the last·day."[15] The moral authority of Scripture is not historically and culturally limited,[16] and for this reason contemporary culture is to be evaluated in the light of Scripture—not vice versa. Therefore, while modern research can facilitate a Christian application of the biblical norms, it cannot be utilized to alter those norms themselves.

In the midst of the current debate over the morality of homosexuality, it also needs to be underscored that the necessary, unquestionable, and relevant law of God is absolute—there are no exceptions that go beyond the text of revealed Scripture. A common sentiment is that, since God's ideal cannot always be achieved in the present sinful world, concessions or exceptions

---

[15]John 12:48.
[16]Isa. 40:8; 1 Pet. 1:24,25; Prov. 14:34; Rom. 2:14,15; Matt. 28:18–20.

must be made in line with man's circumstances and proclivities. If a man finds himself possessed of a homosexual passion, is there not some appropriate—albeit less than ideal—sense in which he can exercise it? Must he be frustrated with unfulfilled physical desires, or is there a possible exception that can be granted? The assumption underlying such questions is that man's imperfections and personal limitations call for a lowering of God's requirements; it is thought that secondary moral demands are suitable enough in Christian ethics when circumstances beyond an individual's control prevent him from full obedience to God's revealed will. This indicates a critical failure to understand the nature of God, whose eyes are too pure to approve evil and who cannot look on wickedness with favor.[17]

God demands in both testaments that men be holy in all manner of behavior: "You shall be holy, for I am holy."[18] Christ settles for no lowering of this unqualified standard of holiness, no rationalizations, no exceptions to God's high demand: "You are to be perfect, even as your heavenly Father is perfect."[19] Therefore, where the law prohibits or commands something, nonscriptural limitations cannot be read into it or excuses made for imperfect performance; the slightest departure from any detail of God's standards renders the offender guilty of the whole law.[20]

The law of God is perfect[21] and as such reflects the nature of God.[22] God alone is good[23] and holy,[24] but because the law expresses His moral character, it too is characterized as good[25] and holy.[26] Doing what is good and right in Jehovah's eyes is

---

[17]Hab. 1:13.
[18]Lev. 11:44f.; 1 Pet. 1:15f.
[19]Matt. 5:48.
[20]James 2:10.
[21]Ps. 19:7; 119:160; Prov. 6:23; Rom. 7:12–25.
[22]Deut. 32:4; Matt. 5:48.
[23]Mark 10:18.
[24]Rev. 15:4.
[25]Mic. 6:8; Rom. 7:12,16; 1 Tim. 1:8.
[26]Rom. 7:12.

observing all His commandments.[27] All these commandments reflect the attributes of God: justice,[28] truth,[29] faithfulness,[30] purity.[31] If these attributes are to be applied to believers as well, it is only as the Holy Spirit fulfills the righteousness of the law in them.[32] This law which bears God's character is revealed consistently throughout Scripture[33] and includes the Mosaic commandments.[34] Our response to this law in Scripture is considered our response to God Himself:[35] the godly man delights in the law[36] even as he delights in the Lord.[37]

Because the law reflects the character of the immutable God,[38] it too is unchangeable. The moral law of God forever binds all persons, believers or not, to obedience. God's commandments are established forever;[39] indeed, every one of His righteous ordinances is everlasting.[40] Consequently, nothing can be subtracted from God's law or ignored.[41] Nor does Christ in the gospel dissolve in any way our responsibility to every word of God's law; rather, He strengthens that obligation. His advent, far from repealing any part of this perfect, good, holy, and unchangeable law, actually reinforces the immutability of God's commandments in full detail:

> Do not think that I have come to abolish the Law or the Prophets; I have not come to abolish them but to fulfill them. I tell you the truth, until

[27]Deut. 12:28.
[28]Ps. 25:8–10; Prov. 28:4,5; Zech. 7:9–12.
[29]Ps. 25:10; 119:142,151; Rev. 15:3.
[30]Ps. 93:5; 111:7; 119:86.
[31]Ps. 119:140.
[32]Rom. 8:4.
[33]Rom. 2:14,15; 5:3; Gen. 6:9,22; 7:1; 26:5; Deut. 8:2; Gal. 3:19; Ps. 119:97,105,106; Isa. 8:16; Hos. 8:12; Mal. 4:4; Matt. 5:16–18; Rom. 3:31; James 1:25; 2:8–11; 1 John 5:3.
[34]Exod. 31:18; Neh. 9:13.
[35]John 12:48; cf. Matt. 5:17–19.
[36]Ps. 1:1,2; 119:16,47.
[37]Ps. 37:4.
[38]Mal. 3:6; James 1:17.
[39]Ps. 111:7; 119:152.
[40]Ps. 119:160.
[41]Deut. 4:2; 12:32; cf. Rev. 22:18,19.

heaven and earth disappear, not the smallest letter, not the least stroke of a pen, will by any means disappear from the Law until everything is accomplished. Anyone who breaks one of the least of these commandments and teaches others to do the same will be called least in the kingdom of heaven.[42]

Therefore, the law of God is perfect and binds everyone to full conformity and to entire obedience forever; what God forbids is never to be done, and what He commands is always our duty. God's law is the absolute standard of holiness and justice, and He cannot tolerate its neglect or violation at any point. The moral law (summarized in the Decalogue and further illustrated in the case laws) is the declaration of God's will to mankind. It directs and binds every one to perpetual obedience in the performance of all those duties that are owed to God and man. Thus God's law stands as a permanently binding norm for personal righteousness and social justice. It is established by faith rather than voided;[43] the believer sees the law as a gracious provision[44] and adheres to it as a result of God's work of grace within him.[45] The law is not burdensome to him[46] but is kept in love[47] and taught according to Christ's direction.[48]

Consequently, the Christian's attitude toward homosexuality must be determined by a faithful study of the infallible Word of God in Scripture, recognizing the law of God as providing authoritative norms for ethics.[49] The present study will try to arrive at conclusions within this biblical framework.

---

[42]Matt. 5:17–19, NIV.

[43]Rom. 3:31.

[44]Ps. 119:29.

[45]Deut. 30:6–8; Ps. 119:166, 174; Jer. 31:33,34; Ezek. 11:19,20; Rom. 6:17–19; Titus 2:11–14.

[46]1 John 5:3.

[47]John 15:10.

[48]Matt. 28:20.

[49]An extensive defense of the normativity of God's law in Christian ethics today can be found in my book, *Theonomy in Christian Ethics* (Nutley, New Jersey: Craig Press, 1977).

2

Homosexuality as a Sin

The preceding discussion has laid the groundwork for a Christian appraisal of homosexuality in response to current challenges. Scripture is received as the self-attesting, fully inspired, infallible Word of God. It is to be interpreted as inerrant, authoritative, and consistent, with careful attention to context, cultural setting, original languages, and Scripture's interpretation of itself. The commandments of God revealed in Scripture are necessary to Christian morality, unquestionable in their requirement, relevant to every age, allowing no extrascriptural exceptions, and perpetually binding. In such a framework, an authentically Christian position regarding homosexuality can be derived. Those who resist the conclusions about homosexuality drawn in this study and who promote contrary attitudes often do so because they are working out of a completely different theological, hermeneutical, or ethical context. Consequently, many contemporary disagreements as to the morality and acceptability (ecclesiastical or civil) of homosexuality can be resolved only at this level. Recognizing this, we can examine now the scriptural materials for their assessment of homosexuality and our response to it. We must turn to the Bible so as to think God's thoughts after Him on this subject.

The Creation Account

When God created the world, He established a fundamental distinction within the human race, reflected in the human body: "male and female created He them."[1] In the creation order upon which God pronounced His benediction,[2] there were but two sexes; the human body was deliberately shaped male (*zakar*) and female (*neqevah*)—the Hebrew words referring specifically to biological, sexual distinction. This natural difference defines and underlies the polarities of man and woman: such a distinction is not an arbitrary accident of evolution (as though survival of the fittest preserved only species able to procreate by couples), nor a mere cultural convention having the force of long-standing tradition. The distinction enunciated in Genesis is more than incidental historical detail. It is a declaration of the proper creation order, cited with authoritative approval and moral significance by Christ.[3] It was God's ordained design for sexual relations to be in the form of male-female union, man and wife becoming "one flesh,"[4] and God created the distinction between the sexes to that end.

This creation of sexual differentiation by God from the beginning established heterosexuality as the normative direction for the sexual impulse and act. God the Creator gives created things their essential identity and function and defines man's proper relationships. Man's sexual function has been defined by God as male-female behavior. This fact refutes the claims of homosexual apologists who say that all human beings have the right to self-

---

[1]Gen. 1:27; cf. 5:2.
[2]Gen. 1:31.
[3]Matt. 19:4.
[4]Gen. 2:24.

definition. Such an existentialist rationale (existence preceding freely chosen essence) reflects an autonomous desire to replace God's intended distinctions and created designs for man with the relativistic will of the creature, who would be worshiped as his own creator.

The opening chapters of the Bible present us with God's original norm that sexual activity was to be within the context of marriage, and they present marriage as exclusively heterosexual in nature. This is true totally apart from any thought that sex and marriage serve solely a procreative function. Man needed a companion and suitable helper,[5] and in response God fashioned a woman from the man; there was unity and distinction. She was called "woman" (*isshah*) precisely because she was taken out of "man" (*ish*);[6] there was common humanity with sexual differentiation. These two creatures were made for each other; their union and interdependence were grounded in the natural order—that is, in their God-given identities and functions.

Marriage, the ordained sphere of sexual relations, is accordingly described as a man and woman "cleaving" to each other and becoming intimately one flesh.[7] This creation ordinance, with its natural differentiation between male and female, is continually reaffirmed by the interpretations of the creation account in the New Testament.[8] Thus Paul maintains that the heterosexual drive is the natural God-given orientation of male and female.[9] Its proper culmination in external expression is reached in marriage, where husband and wife have authority over each other's bodies.[10] Only when sexual impulses are expressed in that specific fashion is the bed undefiled.[11]

---

[5]Gen. 2:18.
[6]Gen. 2:23.
[7]Gen. 2:24.
[8]Mark 10:6–8; 1 Cor. 6:16; Eph. 5:31.
[9]Rom. 1:26,27.
[10]1 Cor. 7:2–5.
[11]Heb. 13:4.

Because man's sexual identity is defined by God, because his orientation is ordained by God, and because his sexual activity is circumscribed within a heterosexual marriage context, homosexuality cannot be viewed merely as a variant sexual preference or accidental variation within creation (akin to lefthandedness). It is not a third natural sex or alternative sexual orientation in God's diverse world. Instead it represents a choice, in some sense, to set one's desires and satisfy one's physical drives in a way contrary to God's appointment and creation. There is no natural homosexuality, for homosexuality is precisely a perversion of nature (understood as God's design for human relations). Homosexuals are made, not born; their disorder is developed contrary to their God-given identity, learned in opposition to the created order, pursued in defiance of the marriage ordinance.

Therefore, where defenders of homosexuality accuse its opponents of secret fears of their own homosexual feelings, of projecting their inability to accept their own desires, they are just rationalizing. In the first place, such a claim rests on the allegation that all adults experience homosexual feelings, which in turn must be defended against counter-evidence by claiming that these feelings are often relegated to an "unconscious level." This way of arguing imposes a contrived theory on the data, a theory which dies the death of a thousand question-begging qualifications.

Ironically, psychological projection may indeed enter the picture here. But given the creation account in Scripture, the projection is that of the homosexual, who projects on the heterosexual his own inability to accept his homosexuality as natural or normal. He cannot genuinely accept his condition, for it defies what God made him to be. The creation account in God's Word undermines the homosexual's defense. Homosexuality, in light of creation, is a severely disordered condition.

Accordingly we conclude that homosexuality cannot be assimilated to the divine order of creation, but belongs to the realm of man's fall into sin. God's will for man is universally heterosexual with respect to sexual expression and activity. In principle, heterosexual marriage is approved within the creation order for man; sins pertaining to heterosexual activity are not sinful simply in virtue of the heterosexual nature of that activity. On the other hand, homosexuality is in principle disapproved by God, for it is contrary to the creation ordinance of marriage; such activity is sinful simply in virtue of its homosexual nature. In the case of heterosexuality, redemption renews and perfects the sexual relations ordained at creation; heterosexual activity—which is indisputably affected by the fall—is sanctified through the redemptive work of the Savior. However, in the case of homosexuality, redemption aims to bring the pursuit of this disorder to a stop, replacing it with the original creation ideal of heterosexual monogamy. Homosexuality is thus contrary to the orders of creation and redemption (re-creation); it is a perverted consequence of man's fall.

The Story of Sodom

The previous judgment is given strong ethical force by the account of Sodom's destruction in Genesis 19. The men of Sodom demanded that two guests of Lot be brought out that the Sodomites might "know" them.[12] The final outcome was that the Sodomites were smitten with blindness and the city divinely destroyed by fire and brimstone. Later biblical references indicate further sins of Sodom which displeased the Lord[13]—even as a

---

[12]Gen. 19:5; Hebrew verb *yadha*.

[13]Ezek. 16:49,50 (which includes the mention of "abomination," cf. Lev. 18:22); it is worth noting however that most references are apparently not *attributing* particular sins to historic Sodom but simply holding up the city as "an example to those who would live ungodly thereafter," as 2 Pet. 2:6 says.

syndrome of unrighteousness is associated with homosexuality in
Paul's mind.[14] Although a general wickedness characterized Sodom,[15] the fact cannot be suppressed that the Sodomites' desire
to "know" Lot's guests is the manifest sin set forth in Genesis 19
and the *specific* confirmation that the city was worthy of devasta-
tion.[16] This was the mark of their extreme degradation and rebellion against God.

What was this sin? Some have suggested that *yadha* is not the
normal word used for homosexual coitus (*shakhabh*) and should
be taken in its ordinary sense of knowing something, thus meaning here "to get acquainted with." The theory is this: as a resident
alien in Sodom, Lot was responsible for introducing his guests to
the townsmen and letting the established citizens examine their
credentials; for that reason the Sodomites asked to "know" Lot's
visitors. They wished to get acquainted with them. Since in the
Hebrew mind a stranger had a right to hospitable reception,[17] the
sin of Sodom would hereby be interpreted as inhospitality to the
visitors.[18] For such a breach of love and social courtesy the Lord
reduced the city to ash.

This theory will not withstand serious scrutiny. In the first
place, Lot was not merely an alien resident in Sodom, but a
prominent social figure "sitting in the gate."[19] He knew well
enough the moral character of the city, so much so that he
became alarmed at the prospect of these visitors spending the
night in a public place and strongly urged them to accept his
invitation of accommodations in his home.[20] When the citizens
later came and asked to "know" his guests, Lot did not see this as

---

[14]Rom. 1:29–31.
[15]Gen. 18:20.
[16]Gen. 19:13; cf. 18:21.
[17]E.g., Gen. 18:1–5; Heb. 13:2.
[18]Cf. Luke 10:10–13, where Jesus linked rejection of His messengers with Sodom's
judgment.
[19]Gen. 19:1.
[20]Gen. 19:2,3.

simply an accepted civil routine whereby visitors have their credentials inspected; he defensively shut the door behind him and characterized the requested "knowing" as a great *wickedness*.[21] It calls for a strange mentality to see (1) how a simple desire of the townsmen to get acquainted would be a breach of hospitality, (2) how it could be deemed seriously wicked (especially in light of the city customs, which Lot certainly understood), and (3) why it would be so vile as to warrant dramatic divine punishment.

Moreover, on this interpretation what would explain Lot's offer to substitute his daughters?[22] The citizens were already acquainted with them; their appearance would have done nothing to prevent the breach of hospitality to Lot's guests. The reply to this objection is that Lot's offer of his daughters was a tempting sexual bribe, intended to appease the crowd and change the subject (away from town protocol regarding visitors). This is psychologically incredible. Why would a father go so far as to propose the violation of his daughters in response to a mere impolite request? Moreover, such a reply requires that we interpret Lot's offer to bring out his daughters "who have not *known* man" as a *sexual* bribe, taking the verb *yadha* to refer to coitus.[23] In that case the same translation should be favored in the immediate context at verse 5 as well; the Sodomites were requesting not mere social acquaintance but sexual relations with Lot's guests—the conclusion this interpretation sought to avoid.

As a final resort, one defender of the reinterpretation of Genesis 19 has suggested that comparison with a similar incident in Judges 19 warrants us to see the intention of the Sodomites as in fact murderous;[24] this accounts for the wickedness perceived by Lot, his extreme preventative offer, and the Lord's wrath at such inhospitality. However, this view suppresses the obvious

---

[21]Gen. 19:6,7.
[22]Gen. 19:8.
[23]As it sometimes does in the Old Testament, e.g., Gen. 4:1.
[24]Note Judg. 20:4–6.

sexual character of the event in Judges 19 and illegitimately
transposes the narrower interpretation onto Genesis 19. It either
exceeds acceptable translations of *yadha* in verse 5, or requires
one to read between the lines of the scriptural account. The
conclusions of such an arbitrary procedure commend themselves
only to those already predisposed to avoid the obvious and natural
meaning of the text.

The men of Sodom desired to have sexual relations with Lot's
visitors, to "know" them. Lot rightly perceived their homosexual
designs as wicked and made his own (unrighteous but contextually appropriate) counteroffer to let these men do as they wished
with his daughters, who had not "known" men (engaged in sexual relations). In the similar story of Judges 19:16ff., the
townsmen of Gibeah surrounded the house of a host, demanding
that his male guest be brought out so that they might "know"
him. Again the request was deemed wicked, and a counterproposal
was made that the guest's concubine be accepted in the place of
their homosexual demands; as a result she was raped until morn-
ing and found dead. In both stories it is clear that the townsmen
were interested in *homosexual* relations, not mere social acquaintance. In the case of Sodom there is no textual reason to view the
intentions of the townsmen specifically as that of homosexual
rape. We have no evidence that they anticipated resistance from
Lot's guests and were seeking sexual assault.

We cannot avoid the obvious conclusion that God devastated
the cities of the plain with a catastrophe because of the homosexuality of the Sodomites. It is pure, ungrounded speculation to
hold that they were punished for an idolatrous fertility cult of
which homosexuality was a part, or for an attempted transgression of the bounds between men and angels; the text has no cultic
indications, nor does it even hint that the Sodomites recognized
Lot's guests as supernatural beings.

Sodom was utterly destroyed because it was a city full of

homosexuals[25] who day after day practiced their impious, sensual debauchery.[26] Unlike many Christians in this secular age, Lot was continually shocked and repulsed ("vexed, tormented") by the lawless deeds of the Sodomites. The use of the word "lawless" (*anomos*) in 2 Peter 2:8 indicates that the Sodomites violated God's command. Even though they were not the elect theocratic people of God, they were responsible to the content of the case law in Leviticus 18:22 and 20:13. The law deep in their heart[27] informed them that those who transgress God's ordinances and practice such things are "worthy of death."[28]

God's inspired Word interprets the Sodom story for us, leaving no doubt that Sodom was devastated for violating God's creation order. In Jude 7 it is precisely the unnaturalness of the vice practiced at Sodom that is stressed as the cause of divine wrath. The Sodomites are there described as "committing fornication and going after strange flesh." The Greek form, *ekporneuein*, is intensive, denoting extravagant lust. The participle, *apelthousai*, adds further intensification and brings out the sense of utter abandonment to impurity. The object of this extravagant, abandoned fornication is said to be *sarkos heteras*, "different flesh." It was *unnatural* sexual intercourse, a departure from the laws of nature (God's ordained pattern for sexual relations), that placed Sodom under God's vengeance.

God's Law

Both the sexual differentiation and marriage ordinance of the creation order and the exceptional destruction of Sodom for its

---

[25]"Young and old, from every end," Gen. 19:4.
[26]2 Pet. 2:6-8.
[27]Rom. 2:14,15.
[28]Rom. 1:32.

homosexuality in the patriarchal period teach the moral prohibition of homosexuality. God condemns homosexuality as unnatural, a severe disorder against creation, and so vile as to warrant death. Creation and history, seen through the spectacles of
God's inspired Word, teach us as much. A direct and specific
formulation of God's prescriptive will for human behavior is
found in the revelation of His law during the Mosaic period; this
sharply defines the moral norms implicit in creation and history.

In the law we learn of the Lord's strong hatred of homosexuality as an abomination. The seventh commandment ("Thou shalt
not commit adultery") protects sexual chastity and the integrity of
the family. It is elaborated and illustrated in various case laws.
Under one commandment in the Decalogue we are to understand that all sins or duties of the same kind are forbidden or
commanded, together with all the causes, means, occasions, and
provocations thereto. The general moral equity of these judicial
laws is that of the original, foundational requirement of the Ten
Commandments; they cannot be dismissed as lacking validity
today.[29] Therefore, one of the sins forbidden in the seventh
commandment is sodomy and all unnatural lusts: "You shall not
lie with a male as with a woman; it is an abomination."[30] "If a
man lies with a male as with a woman, both of them have
committed an abomination; they shall be put to death, their
bloodguiltiness is upon them."[31]

God's verdict on homosexuality is inescapably clear. His law is
a precise interpretation of the sexual order of creation for fallen
man, rendering again His intention and direction for sexual relations. When members of the same sex (*homo*-sexual) practice
intercourse with each other (expressed by the idiom "to lie with,"
shakar eth), they violate God's basic creation order in a vile or
abominable fashion. Throughout Leviticus we see God's absolute

---

[29]Cf. Matt. 5:17–48; 1 Cor. 9:8–10; 2 Cor. 6:14; 1 Tim. 5:18; Mark 10:19.
[30]Lev. 18:22.
[31]Lev. 20:13.

standards for purity; in the sexual realm one may not profanely use the creation of God, "uncovering the nakedness" of man, woman, or beast indiscriminately.[32] Sexual relations must be conducted within God-given boundaries.

What was revealed in the creation account and the history of Sodom has been confirmed in statutory form. The Lord will not tolerate homosexuality. However, it is not surprising that those who suppress the implications of sexual differentiation at creation and who reinterpret the sin of Sodom have also attempted to mitigate the condemnation of God's law regarding homosexuality.

Some attempts are hardly worth refuting. We are told that love is the only issue in any sexual relationship, and therefore it would be submitting to a double standard of morality for the Christian to condone heterosexual love-making and condemn homosexual love-making. God surely would not expect the manner of attaining sexual gratification to be made important, setting down a standard that commends one sexual preference while condemning another. Such a rationale not only ignores the specific revelation of God in Leviticus 18:22 and 20:13, where it is clear that God does indeed regard the specific manner of one's sexual gratification to be morally important, but also it easily can be reduced to absurdity (e.g., "surely God would not have a double standard regarding the attainment of money, distinguishing between work and theft").

Others have argued that the prohibition of homosexuality is rooted in the arbitrariness of the Jewish people regarding sexual matters, and that there is no reason for it in terms of social consequences (i.e., it does not harm society or violate the rights of others). Such thinking contradicts the divine authorship of the law.[33] If, contrary to the views of Jesus and Paul,[34] the moral

---

[32]Cf. Lev. 18; 20.
[33]Cf. Lev. 18:1–5.
[34]Cf. Matt. 22:39,40; John 10:35; 2 Tim. 3:16,17.

code of Leviticus 18–20 is not received as inspired of God, then it is superfluous to debate its binding character. But if it is deemed to be divine in origin, then it is arbitrary on the part of the critic to renounce the sections unfavorable to his preconceived notions.

Presumably there are good social reasons for the laws that confine sexual relations to heterosexual marriage. God's Word says that they are laid down for our positive good.[35] The blessings of obedience and the curses of disobedience are momentous.[36] Any other attitude would certainly lead to a permissiveness toward sex that would degrade and destroy the integrity of the family. However, we would be bound to God's law regarding homosexuality even if we could not see its positive social consequences. The goal of our ethical system is not to satisfy the tastes of the creature, but to please the Creator and reflect His absolute holiness.

More serious challenges to the apparent meaning of the laws against homosexuality in Leviticus have been leveled: namely, that they are ceremonial (and thus temporary), or that they are simply circumstantial (i.e., condemning the associations and uses of homosexuality in ancient society). The first argument is that the injunctions of Leviticus 18:22 and 20:13 appear in connection with cultic purification and thus belong to the "shadows" of the ceremonial law dispelled by fulfillment in Christ. Therefore it would be inconsistent to apply Leviticus's prohibitions of homosexuality today while rejecting Leviticus's prohibition, for example, of unclean meats.[37] Now it is true that the covenant of grace was administered differently before and after Christ's coming. Some Old Testament laws served primarily not to define sin and its just sanctions but to reveal by means of types the way of redemptive restoration to God's favor. Under the Old Testament

---

[35]Deut. 6:24; 10:13; 30:15,19,20; 32:46,47.
[36]Cf. Deut. 28.
[37]Lev. 20:25.

dispensation God's gracious covenant was administered by promises, prophecies, sacrifices, circumcision, the passover lamb, and other types and ordinances delivered to the Jews; they were "the gospel in figures," signifying Christ and His redemptive work.[38]

These ceremonial laws have all been fulfilled for the believer by Christ's obedience, so the covenant of grace under the gospel is administered now through preaching and the sacraments. The ceremonial laws God gave Israel, containing several typical ordinances prefiguring Christ, His graces, actions, sufferings and benefits, have all under the New Testament been "put out of gear."[39] This distinction between moral and ceremonial laws is not arbitrary. It has a rationale required by Scripture as it interprets itself: moral law defines justice while ceremonial law guides redemptive restoration.

Therefore, we recognize the category of temporary, ceremonial law in the Old Testament. However, there is no good reason to assign the prohibitions of homosexuality to it. They do not anticipate the person and work of Christ for salvation in any sense. Further, the fact that homosexuality was to receive the death penalty in Israel places it in the sphere of other moral offenses punished by the Jewish magistrate, not in the sphere of temporary ceremonial legislation.

Moreover, the context of these prohibitions suggests that they pertain to moral holiness, not mere cultic purification. The list of injunctions in Leviticus 18 is introduced with emphatic divine authority: "You are to perform my judgments and keep my statutes, to walk in them; I am the Lord your God;[40] it ends, "Thus you are to keep my charge. . . . I am the Lord your God."[41] The next chapter contains further laws, introduced with these words: "You shall be holy, for I the Lord your God am

---

[38]Cf. Heb. 8:5; 10:1.
[39]Cf. Heb. 7:11,12,28; 8:13; 10:8,9; Eph. 2:14–16.
[40]Lev. 18:4.
[41]Lev. 18:30.

holy";[42] it ends, "You shall thus observe all my statutes, and all my ordinances, and do them: I am the Lord."[43] Chapter 20 is a continuation of such injunctions: "Then the Lord spoke to Moses, saying, 'You shall also say to the sons of Israel . . .'";[44] it similarly ends, "Thus you are to be holy to me, for I the Lord am holy."[45]

In contrast to such ethical requirements reflecting the lordship and holiness of God, chapter 21 begins a new section dealing with requirements for priests and their cultic service. The preceding passage[46] contains some requirements that are no longer observed in their Jewish form, e.g., those which symbolize the separation of Israel from the abominations committed by her pagan neighbors[47] and a few ceremonial instructions.[48] But the predominant character of its commandments is moral, and their content is generally recognized as binding today (e.g., prohibiting incest, adultery, child sacrifice, idolatry, oppression of the poor, slander, hatred, unjust weights and measures). Christ Himself appealed to them as summarizing all the law and the prophets.[49]

Therefore, the context does not support the automatic dismissal of the prohibitions against homosexuality as ceremonial. The defender of homosexuality must produce a viable criterion for distinguishing between moral and ceremonial laws, or else consistently reject them all (contrary to the emphatic word of Christ). We have New Testament warrant for discontinuing obedience to the sacrificial system,[50] and the failure to observe the symbols of separation from the Gentile no longer displeases God.[51] How-

---

[42]Lev. 19:2.
[43]Lev. 19:37.
[44]Lev. 20:1,2.
[45]Lev. 20:26.
[46]Lev. 18–20.
[47]Cf. Lev. 18:3,24–30; 19:19; 20:22–26.
[48]Lev. 19:5–8,21,22.
[49]Lev. 19:18; cf. Matt. 22:39,40.
[50]Heb. 10:1–18.
[51]Acts 10:9–20.

ever, the Scriptures never alter God's revealed law regarding homosexuality, but leave us under its full requirement.[52] Indeed, the Bible repeatedly condemns homosexuality, the New Testament itself stressing that it is contrary to God's law,[53] bringing God's judgment and exclusion from the kingdom.[54] Therefore, the prohibition against homosexuality cannot be viewed as part of the ceremonial system prefiguring Christ or as temporary in its obligation.

Another attempt to loosen the binding character of the prohibition of homosexuality in God's law reinterprets the prohibition as dealing with homosexuality's aggravating circumstances and not with homosexuality as such, independent of its ancient associations or social implications. One reinterpretation maintains that in the Jewish mind homosexuality was associated with the idolatry of Israel's neighbors, who practiced cultic fertility rites in their temples, using male and female prostitutes. Thus the Holiness Code in Leviticus, which (as we have noted above) warned repeatedly against the idolatrous practices of the Canaanites, should be seen as condemning cultic homosexuality. This connection is explicit in Deuteronomy 23:17,18, where it is prohibited for the sons of Israel to become cult prostitutes and thereby bring the wages of a "dog" into the Lord's house.[55] This derisive term indicates how abominable this was to God. It is also clear from Israel's later history that such cultic homosexuality was a moral problem for that society.[56]

By association, then, the prohibition of homosexuality becomes in fact a metaphorical prohibition of idolatry; it was revealed in order to keep the Israelites from contact with alien religions, which practiced cultic defilement, homosexual fertility

---

[52]Cf. Deut. 8:3; 12:32; Matt. 4:4.
[53]1 Tim. 1:9,10.
[54]Rom. 1:24ff.; 1 Cor. 6:9,10.
[55]Cf. Rev. 22:15.
[56]Cf. 1 Kings 14:23,24; 15:12; 22:46; 2 Kings 23:7; Hos. 4:14.

rites as part of their idolatrous worship. In this way the prohibition against lying with a man as one does with a woman[57] is taken in the same way as the prohibition of boiling a kid in its mother's milk,[58] namely as forbidding participation in what historical research has shown to be heathen religious practices. In this connection it could be observed that the verse immediately preceding Leviticus 18:22 mentions an obvious idolatrous practice of the Canaanites (child sacrifice to Molech), and it has been speculated that the verse immediately following (prohibiting the perversion of bestiality) refers to an Egyptian goat cult and/or Canaanite heifer cult. Hence God's law against homosexuality is circumstantial and has nothing to say about homosexuality in non-cultic contexts.

Another reinterpretation attributes prohibitions to the procreative emphasis among the Jews, who saw childlessness as a spiritual curse and/or an economic hardship and who viewed the willful destruction of viable human semen as a serious crime.[59] Thus homosexuality was actually prohibited because it was impossible through such sexual activity to propagate the chosen race.

Another reinterpretation claims that in the ancient world homosexual rape was inflicted upon a defeated male enemy as a symbol of domination and an expression of scorn (as in the Egyptian epic, *The Contending of Horus and Seth*). Therefore the Jewish law prohibited homosexuality as a sign of disrespect for a person and a dishonoring of the superior male gender (which was reduced to the performance of a female function). In these views, the biblical prohibition would have no continuing moral force outside of cultures that insist on procreation as the key function of sexual relations or that see homosexuality as a symbol of scorn and dishonor.

---

[57]Lev. 18:22.
[58]Exod. 23:19.
[59]As seen in the Onan story, Gen. 38:8–10.

What can be said about these various circumstantial reinterpretations of the biblical prohibition of homosexuality? First, they are not consistent with each other; an act of religious worship, a failure to pursue the best end for man, and a positive act of scornful domination are completely different and incompatible things. The circumstantial reinterpreters of the biblical prohibition against homosexuality need to resolve their own disagreement as to what the law "really" meant to forbid. Without a clear candidate for the sin which actually stands behind the apparent meaning of Leviticus 18:22 in its alleged cultural setting, there is no serious challenge to which we must respond.

More importantly, these theories, one and all, do not warrant any definite conclusion about what is actually prohibited when God speaks of homosexuality; at best they are speculative searches for what might possibly be an underlying rationale for the prohibition of homosexuality. And at many points they are not even very plausible possibilities.

The "homosexuality-as-scorn" theory rests on pure conjecture as to the meaning of the biblical texts themselves.[60] Moreover, the idea that homosexuality represents a willing submission to a scornful and dishonorable manner of behavior does not detract from the traditional understanding of the biblical prohibition in the least, but supplements it.

The "homosexuality-as-contrary-to-procreation" theory completely overlooks the fact that sexual relations served an essential role in man's need for human companionship, not simply procreation, in the Old Testament theology of marriage.[61] The allegation that Hebrews viewed semen as somehow sacred rests on a complete misreading of the Onan story, for Onan was punished for a violation of the levirate institution and not simply for wasting his seed. Homosexuality was punished as a positive

---

[60] Or else an illegitimate interpolation of Gen. 9:22.
[61] Cf. Gen. 2:19–25.

sin of commission, not merely as the failure to generate children through one's sexual activities. Otherwise heterosexual barrenness would be similarly condemned.

Such imaginative views are not based on an exegetical study of the Bible's own teaching but are imposed from outside. Scripture's own inspired rationale for God's prohibition of homosexuality is simple and direct: "It is an abomination (*toevah*),"[62] that is, detestable in the sight of God, loathed as degrading and offensive to the moral sense.

Of course it might be idolatrous abomination, as the first circumstantial reinterpretation of the prohibition suggested. The problems with this theory, however, are textual and historical. God's Word contains a separate and explicit prohibition of cultic homosexuality,[63] whereas in Leviticus 18:22 there is no reference to cult prostitutes and thus no necessary association with idolatrous rites.

The prohibition in Leviticus is found in a context predominately moral in character (as discussed above). The alleged cultic character of verse 23 is entirely speculative, and even the idolatrous reference in verse 21 does not make that particular command any less moral in its intention. After all, the prohibition of child sacrifice serves to protect human life and prevent the destruction of the family, as well as shunning pollution with Canaanite idolatry; the fact that this sin was historically a cultic rite does not make it any less a perpetual moral issue. The point, then, is that Leviticus 18:22 is distinct from the law against cultic homosexuality; the contexts of the two prohibitions are different, and there is no suggestion of idolatrous sexual rites in the Leviticus passage.

The appeal to historical and cultural background will do nothing to remedy this defect; in fact, it will defeat the theory altogether. The historical fact is that in Canaanite culture homosexuality was practiced as both a religious rite and a personal

---

[62]Lev. 18:22.
[63]Deut. 23:17,18.

sexual perversion in general; it was popular in the temple and the town, performed both religiously and hedonistically. Israel's pagan neighbors knew both secular and sacred homosexuality, which would make two different biblical prohibitions all the more necessary for God's will to be clearly revealed to His people. The Bible condemns the sex life of the heathen town as well as the sexual idolatry of the heathen temple.

The advocates of the circumstantial reinterpretation of Leviticus 18:22 and 20:13 do not prove that these verses must be interpreted as saying what Deuteronomy 23:17,18 says and no more. In fact they illegitimately collapse the two distinct prohibitions into each other, thereby suppressing a portion of God's moral will—as does an interpreter who reads Romans 13:13 and 1 Corinthians 11:21 and concludes that God merely forbids drunkenness at the sacraments of the church and not drunkenness in general.

Even if it could be shown that there is some cultic association with the homosexuality prohibited in Leviticus 18:22, there is still no reason to think that the law is exhaustively cultic in its reference; after all, God would abhor homosexuality all the more, it seems, for its incidental idolatrous connections. The circumstance would in this sense aggravate the offense of homosexuality, not reformulate the basic meaning of the prohibition.

The error of this circumstantial reinterpretation of Leviticus 18:22 is all the more clear when one realizes that the same line of interpretation could be applied to the prohibition of bestiality in verse 23. Parallel reasoning would lead us to deem bestiality outside of religious or cultic contexts as morally acceptable today—a conclusion that ought to shock our ethical sensibilities (even if we have become insensitive to the continual propaganda for homosexuality in present-day culture).

Many counterexamples to the pattern of argument used in the circumstantial reinterpretation undermine its validity and credibility. For example, the historical fact that stealing is always associated with envy or covetousness, which is idolatry according to Colossians 3:5, would not *reduce* the eighth commandment to the second or tenth.

Homosexuality is so vile in God's sight, so repugnant to His moral character, that in ancient Israel it carried the sanction of capital punishment.[64] We must remember that in the Old Testament "every transgression and disobedience received a just recompense."[65] Homosexuality is so contrary to creation and to God's will that every hint of wiping out the created distinction between the sexes was also forbidden. Even impersonating the other sex by one's clothing was abominable.[66]

Homosexuality is presented in God's just law as worthy of death. Now with other capital crimes the law of God draws important ethical distinctions relating, for example, to the offender's motivation[67] or the circumstances of the offense.[68] When qualifications and mitigating circumstances are relevant in evaluating the crime, God lays them down for us and does not leave them to speculation and later historical research. But no excuse, amendment, or circumstantial consideration mitigated the prohibition or punishment of homosexuality. The instructions for the severe sanction against it in Israel were simple and direct. Under no circumstances could homosexuality be tolerated as morally acceptable.

Therefore we are compelled to say that God's law against homosexuality cannot be deprived of its force. It is not an objectionable double standard, is not arbitrary and inconsequential, cannot be taken as a temporary ceremonial law, and ought not to be reduced to circumstantial sins associated with it or its social

---

[64]Lev. 20:13.
[65]Heb. 2:2.
[66]Deut. 22:5.
[67]E.g., murder: Deut. 19:4–13.
[68]E.g., rape: Deut. 22:23–29.

implications. The numerous attempts to escape its binding character are futile and lead to the distortion of God's Word through interpretive methods that must read things into the text, ignore the broader context of Scripture, violate the analogy of faith, and resort to fallacious maneuvers.

God has created man in such a way and ordered social relations in such a way, God has worked such judgment in the course of history, God has such a holy character as is transcribed in the law, that homosexuality is "an abomination." It upsets the proper sexual relations between people, representing an attempt to redefine man and the world in the image of the sinner. It provokes the wrath of God, is diametrically opposed to His nature, and is punishable by death. This much is taught in the creation account, the story of Sodom, and the law of God.

It was because the Canaanites practiced such "abominations" as homosexuality that God scourged them from the land.[69] This shows that the Mosaic law's content was binding even on those *outside* the covenant community, those not given the redemptive special revelation of God's law—a fact that confutes the suggestion that God's law cannot have direct binding force in the modern secular state, but only in the church of Christ. All men in all times and all cultures are obligated by the Lord to abhor and refrain from homosexuality. From the perspective of Old Testament revelation the conclusion is clear: homosexuality is perverted (contrary to God's created order), immoral (contrary to God's commandment), and worthy of death (temporal, societal, eternal).

Romans 1

Identical principles are authoritatively revealed in the first chapter of Paul's Epistle to the Romans, thus providing explicit

---

[69]Lev. 18:24–30.

New Testament confirmation of the Old Testament ethic regarding homosexuality.

> For this reason God gave them over to degrading passions; for their
> women exchanged the natural function for that which is unnatural, and
> in the same way also the men abandoned the natural function of the
> woman and burned in their desire towards one another, men with men
> committing indecent acts and receiving in their own persons the due
> penalty of their error. . . . And although they know the ordinance of God,
> that those who practice such things [the sins listed in verses 28-31] are
> worthy of death, they not only do the same, but also give hearty approval
> to those who practice them.[70]

In this context Paul was teaching that the wrath of God is
revealed from heaven against those who turn from their proper
relationship to the Creator; suppressing the truth of God, they
resort to various forms of idolatry, serving the creature with darkened minds and foolish reasoning. In response, God gives them
over to impure lusts and the dishonoring of their bodies—
specifically, to homosexuality, which in turn stimulates further
depravities. Men who give up God and His law are eventually
given up by God to wander in morally polluted practices that
become a way of life. Specifically, the penalty for man's rebellion
against the true service to God is homosexuality, which Paul
described with reinforcing disapprobation as "impurity," "dishonoring of the body,"[71] "degrading passions,"[72] "indecent acts"
(or "shameless deeds"), "error,"[73] the "improper" activity of a
"depraved mind."[74] Homosexuality exchanges the natural use of
sex for unnatural sexual practices,[75] thereby evidencing immoral
perversion in the most intimate of human relations and being

---

[70]Rom. 1:26,27,32, NASB.
[71]Rom. 1:24.
[72]Rom. 1:26.
[73]Rom. 1:27.
[74]Rom. 1:28.
[75]Rom. 1:26,27.

"worthy of death."[76] The best commentary on this teaching is found in the Old Testament, upon which Paul drew heavily.

Scripture's most obvious condemnation of homosexuality as intrinsically immoral is found in this Romans passage. Nevertheless, there are those who seek to evade its straightforward indictment. In the first place there are those who maintain that Paul did not single out homosexuality as especially offensive among sins; it is not taken up as a subject in its own right but merely dealt with incidentally among the results of a perverted relationship to God—presented simply as part of a broader pattern of pagan excesses.

Such a response to Paul's words is plainly wrong. After all, homosexuality is presented precisely as an appropriate illustration of sinful depravity. Indeed, it is Paul's key illustration of the perversion that results from rebellion against God, a conspicuous symptom of such rebellion. The subject is discussed, to be sure, in relation to its roots and effects, but the moral character of homosexuality is nonetheless discussed in its own right as well. Its vile character clinches Paul's argument concerning the consequences of suppressing the knowledge of God, and thus what Paul said in describing it cannot be minimized. To contend that homosexuality in Romans 1 is portrayed merely as a punishment for sin and not as a sin itself is to forget that God often punishes sin by turning men over to that sin and its effects completely.[77] This is exactly what Paul said about homosexuality: it is both sin and punishment for sin.[78]

Second, there are supporters of homosexuality who claim that Paul is condemning lust and promiscuity, not homosexual love and devotion; the assumption is that the moral quality of homosexuality cannot be judged in isolation from the attitude

---

[76]Rom. 1:32.
[77]E.g., Hos. 4:17.
[78]Cf. Rom. 1:24.

and context in which one exercises it, the interpersonal support it supplies, and the personal fulfillment it offers. Supposedly there are distinctions to be drawn, with the result that we should recognize a commendable Christian practice of homosexuality in contrast to depraved versions of it.

But such a suggestion is mere wishful thinking without biblical support. Paul was quite adept at drawing careful moral distinctions. He recognized pertinent qualifications that had to be made and gave his readers details of intricate ethical problems (such as those regarding meats offered to idols, marriage and divorce, spiritual gifts, exhortations and rebukes, uses and abuses of the law). If homosexuality could gain divine approval in any sense, Paul would have indicated as much and drawn the distinctions which men now wish to impose upon his text.

In ancient culture homosexuality was commonplace, with certain distinctions customarily drawn between homosexuality as an ideal expression of love (e.g., in Plato's *Symposium*) or an aid to military prowess (e.g., in Spartan propaganda) and homosexuality in the form of prostitution and indiscriminate infatuation. The one was encouraged, the other discouraged. By contrast, Paul, who was well versed in the culture of his day, drew no such distinctions but categorically condemned homosexuality without exception. Scripture cannot be interpretively shaped to fit the contours of sin, and homosexuality cannot be cleverly domesticated within a divinely approved lifestyle. There is no more a Christian form of homosexuality than there is a Christian form of adultery or bestiality or rape, etc. Romans 1 makes no room for any kind of homosexuality whatsoever, for it is plainly and simply "error," a *wrong* lifestyle.[79] If Paul's words can be twisted to allow for homosexuality under certain conditions, the same line of thought can be taken with all of the sins elaborated in verses 28–31—indeed, with any sin whatsoever!

---

[79]Rom. 1:27.

The third attempt to blunt Paul's condemnation of homosexuality argues that Paul's fundamental concern was the general influence of paganism on believers or the contaminating idolatry of Hellenistic cultures, which was associated with homosexuality in the mind of any pious Jew (and which would be a particular problem for Roman Christians). One author goes so far as to say that Romans 1:26–31 is merely Paul's cliché-ridden summary of a well-known list of vices popularly used to condemn Gentile culture and religion. Since Paul's intention was simply to use such a hackneyed catalogue to say that all men[80] fall under the rule of God's wrath, we must conclude that there is nothing particularly virtuous about any sexual orientation in itself, heterosexual or homosexual. One would also fall under Paul's condemnation in Romans 1 by insisting upon—and thereby idolizing—the sexual preference of heterosexuality. It also represents worship of the creature rather than the Creator, failing to see God's gracious acceptance in the face of man's rejection (the theme of the epistle). So then, a true understanding of Paul's teaching would allow one to be "graciously gay," we are told.

At some point in a discussion such as this it becomes appropriate to warn interpreters of God's inspired Word that they must be careful not to "wrest the Scriptures unto their own destruction."[81] The preceding misstatement of Paul's teaching is a dangerous perversion of the biblical doctrines of God's wrath and grace. To say that all men are condemned by God's law is not at all the same as saying that God's law condemns all attitudes and behavior; there are actions which God commands (e.g., working gainfully six days a week) and which God condemns (e.g., stealing, Sabbath-breaking), even though no man perfectly abides by God's will in these matters.

Paul cited homosexuality as a specific violation of God's re-

---

[80]Gentile as well as Jewish: Rom. 1; 2.
[81]2 Pet. 3:16.

vealed will in his conclusion that all men are condemned by the law. But men's universal condemnation under law cannot be used to empty specific commands of their content, making heterosexuality and homosexuality equally sinful in God's sight. Likewise, the insistence on upholding God's moral standard (e.g., regarding heterosexuality) over against its transgression can be deemed idolatrous only by eliminating any thought of clear and definable moral character in God. The grace of God teaches men to renounce sin and live by the righteous pattern of God's law; for that reason one can be "graciously gay" no more than one can "graciously murder." We must beware of such "ungodly persons who turn the grace of our God into licentiousness."[82]

If Paul drew from a well-known list of pagan vices in Romans 1, then we should conclude that indeed these are, in God's sight, genuine vices. The fact that a biblical writer had historical sources for his own teaching[83] does not undermine the accuracy of what he taught,[84] for men moved by the Holy Spirit spoke from God and the final product of their efforts must be accounted as God-breathed.[85] However, in light of our previous investigation and Paul's specific vocabulary, it is much more likely that Paul's particular starting point for his teaching about homosexuality was the Old Testament.

The fact that Paul moved in Romans 1 directly from a discussion of idolatry to homosexuality does not suggest that he was referring exclusively to cultic homosexuality. As similarly discussed regarding Old Testament law, Romans does not specify cultic prostitution, and in terms of historical setting there would be every reason for Paul to condemn secular homosexuality itself (and not merely cultic homosexuality).

---

[82]Jude 4.
[83]E.g., Luke 1:3.
[84]Luke 1:4.
[85]2 Pet. 1:21; 2 Tim. 3:16.

Paul's words in Romans 1 cannot be restricted to the pagans' ritual homosexuality any more than his judgment on prostitution[86] can be restricted to the well-known occurrences of this sin within pagan cultic services. Verses 28–31 indicate clearly that Paul's mind was on intrinsically moral behavior as he discussed repercussions of abandoning the knowledge of God.[87] Furthermore, it is evident from the text that Paul was not simply concerned with the general influence of paganism or with merely expressing a narrow-minded disdain for Hellenistic culture. He dealt bluntly and specifically with homosexuality as the manifest outcome of paganism and the leading proof of the degradation of Hellenistic culture; the other sins mentioned are accompanying vices to homosexuality. The offense was not its Greek background (which was hardly unique) but its transgression of God's holy standards of morality revealed in nature and Scripture.

The last attempt to dispose of Paul's condemnation of homosexuality that we shall investigate, by far the most ingenious, is the claim that Paul was condemning perversion and not inversion. Some allege that Romans 1:26,27 describes people who "exchange" their own natural inclination toward heterosexuality for homosexuality, thereby perverting their own nature; it does not touch on the inverted person who has never been attracted to the opposite sex and is by his own nature homosexually inclined. This would mean that those who are (according to the theory) constitutionally homosexual in their orientation and who have not willfully given up their natural sexual relations for what would be "unnatural" to them (heterosexuality) do not come within the scope of Paul's judgment. Indeed, we are told that it would be perverted according to Paul's teaching for a naturally oriented homosexual to turn to heterosexuality in his behavior, for that

---

[86]1 Cor. 6:15.

[87]Note the similar introductions to verses 26,27 regarding homosexuality and verses 29–31 regarding a variety of immoral deeds and attitudes.

would be an exchange from the natural to the unnatural. It turns out that what was apparently the strongest indication of homosexuality's intrinsic immorality becomes in fact the homosexual's greatest defense!

This defense rests on the interpretation it offers of the phrase "against nature" (*para phusin*) in verse 26. Not a few defenders of homosexuality fluctuate between contrary approaches to the phrase, and some try to combine senses in which it might be taken so as to exonerate "constitutional" homosexuality in one way or another. For purposes of analysis it will be best to isolate the options that have been suggested, finally returning specifically to the above theory.

(1) According to one approach, Paul was speaking of what is contrary to the intrinsic nature or essence of a thing;[88] however, Paul's judgment against homosexuality cannot be taken at face value, for what is and is not "natural" cannot be clearly established or conclusively evaluated. How does one discern that something or someone is acting "contrary to nature"—by statistical comparison with others (in which case the "natural" constantly changes), or by perceiving an individual's own common pattern (in which case systematic behavior can never be perverse)? Do we want to condemn homogenized milk simply on the grounds that it is unnatural?

(2) Another approach reads Paul as speaking of that which is contrary to a religio-cultural heritage or custom, matters of training and social conditioning; for a Jew what is "against nature" would be functionally equivalent to what is improper by Jewish custom and forbidden to the chosen people in God's law.[89] Thus in Romans 1:26 Paul was simply making the point that the Gentiles go beyond what was approved for the Jews in Leviticus because the Gentiles have not recognized the living and true God.

---

[88]As in Rom. 11:24, where the ingrafting of tree branches is said to be "against nature."

[89]Cf. Gal. 2:15 where those who are Jews "by nature" have a manner of life distinct from the Gentiles, who are "by nature" uncircumcised, according to Rom. 2:27.

Homosexuality is not being viewed as evil independent of a person's social customs but only within the context of Jewish law, which saw it as an expression of cultic idolatry.

(3) Finally, others think that in speaking of behavior "against nature" Paul had in mind a conscious choice to act contrary to one's normal inclinations. Paul censures men for engaging in sexual acts that are contrary to their ordinary heterosexual appetites, but does not speak to the question of inversion (a psychological condition wherein one is naturally inclined toward members of the same sex) because it does not reflect an *abandoning* of one's own natural function.[90]

In reply to the first suggestion and its critical attack on the possibility of knowing and evaluating what is "natural," we need simply observe that God, the Creator of man, who establishes the essence of all things and ordained man's normal functions, is certainly in a position to reveal what is natural to sexual relations. While in some respects He requires man to use, subdue, and change the natural world (e.g., removing weeds, curing polio), He nevertheless forbids the transgression of certain essential boundaries.[91] Despite the problems of a philosophy of natural law that is devised independently of God's revelation, the fact remains that God knows the essential nature of all things and thus can infallibly declare the appropriate functions and relations for man.

In reply to the second suggestion, we must remember that the Jewish law of the Old Testament is still normative for the modern world. It was not intended as an ethical eccentricity of the Israelites but is manifest in the hearts of the Gentiles,[92] stands as an ideal and standard for all nations,[93] and shows how God's kingdom comes and His will is done on earth as it is in heaven. Accordingly, even if Paul meant in Romans 1:26 that homosexu-

---

[90]Cf. Rom. 1:27a, where the punctiliar aorist participle, *aphentes*, could suggest a specific past point of transition from heterosexual to homosexual activity.

ality was contrary to the "customary" Jewish law (i.e., nature), this would not mitigate his universal condemnation of it. Moreover, as was discussed previously, the Jewish law does not condemn homosexuality simply in terms of idolatrous circumstances; it prohibits all forms of homosexuality, secular and sacred.

In reply to all three suggestions, but more particularly to the third, we need to observe the proper meaning of Paul's words, "against nature." In the immediate context we note that Paul is speaking of the knowledge of God available to men through the created world, rendering them without excuse in failing to glorify God properly and in exchanging the truth for a lie.[94] Moreover, there is an internal witness to the moral standards of God in every man.[95] Men are responsible to know certain things from the objective condition or order of the world and human nature; therefore Scripture can speak of nature teaching obvious moral truths,[96] of men understanding things naturally or instinctively,[97] and of men by nature doing the things of God's law.[98]

In the New Testament the "natural" pertains to the *created world* and its present general order as ordained by God, ranging from ordinary living things such as animals[99] or branches[100] and biological processes,[101] to the fundamental, original condition of things without artificial intervention—either their *innate* character[102] or *inherited* condition.[103] God has ordained "the natural

---

[91]E.g., nothing in the created realm is to be worshiped, for the Creator alone is God by nature, Gal. 4:8; it is natural that there be a recognized distinction between the sexes, 1 Cor. 11:14.

[92]Rom. 2:14,15.

[93]Deut. 4:8; Isa. 51:4; Lev. 18:24–27; Prov. 14:34; Ps. 72:1–11; Matt. 28:18–20.

[94]Rom. 1:18–25.

[95]Rom. 2:14,15.

[96]1 Cor. 11:14.

[97]Jude 10.

[98]Rom. 2:14.

[99]James 3:7; 2 Pet. 2:12.

[100]Rom. 11:21,24.

[101]Rom. 11:24.

[102]Gal. 4:8; James 3:7; 2 Pet. 1:4.

[103]Gal. 2:15; Rom. 2:27; Eph. 2:3.

function" for sexual relations in His creation order: the normal, and normative, pattern of male and female becoming one flesh. God's creation ordinance, with the specific distinction between male and female, intended for heterosexual relations to be "natural." Man's inherited condition and ordinary biological process, the essential character of his sexuality when there is no artificial intervention and willful reorientation, is therefore heterosexual. This information is clearly known from creation and conscience by those who disorder the natural function of sex.[104] There is in the biblical perspective no such thing as "natural homosexuality." It is always at base a perversion of the created order.

To interpret the phrase "exchanged the natural function for that which is against nature" as pertaining to the personal, psycho-sexual orientation of individuals or the particular biographical history of certain people who go from one kind of sexual activity to another requires forced exegesis. Paul spoke, not of one's personal and previous sexual engagements, but of "the natural function"—regardless of whether individual homosexuals have in fact consciously experienced heterosexual desires or acts. His thrust was that men and women have departed from what is natural for mankind, not for individual persons. His discussion was generic and categorical, dealing with the sexual function that God has ordained as natural for man, not with the individualized sexual natures of diverse individuals. Homosexuals "exchange" the right way to gain sexual gratification for one which is *in itself* "against nature";[105] what males are said to "abandon" is not their own personal customary sexual activity but rather "the natural use of the female."[106] It may be in some sense individually "natural" for someone to be a kleptomaniac, but it is nonetheless a perversion of God's will for man's prescribed manner of obtain-

---

[104]Rom. 1:32; cf. 1:19,20; 2:14,15.
[105]Rom. 1:26.
[106]Rom. 1:27.

ing things. Likewise, to say that heterosexual desires and acts are not "natural" to those individuals who are (allegedly) constitutionally homosexual plainly suppresses Paul's point. Homosexuality *per se* is always unnatural.

It is artificial to argue that Paul's verb tense in the phrase "abandoned the natural function" was chosen to denote exclusively an explicit act of renouncing former heterosexual ways by the homosexual. Rather, the verb signifies a resultant condition, not a conscious and definite act of past sexual conversion; (the connotation of past time is not necessary to the aorist participle at all). What Paul was teaching is the simple fact that those who burn with homosexual desire and commit indecent acts have effectively abandoned what God ordained for man's natural sexual impulse.

Therefore, this last attempt to dispose of Paul's condemnation of homosexuality fails as did the others. An exclusion of alleged inverts cannot be read into the text, setting them apart from Paul's censure of others who practice homosexual deeds after involvement in heterosexual patterns. Paul's simple point is that homosexuality in itself has the wrong sexual object. All homosexuality, regardless of whether one is inverted or converted to homosexuality, is itself a perversion, a departure from God's ordained use of sex. No qualifying or mitigating distinctions are warranted textually or theologically. The creation order and the law of God have been violated in any and all expressions of homosexuality.

As indicated previously, these emphases of Paul are based on the teaching of the Old Testament. The creation account establishes heterosexuality as the pattern of man's sexual activity and desire; accordingly, Paul viewed homosexuality as an exchange of the natural for that which is against nature.[107] The Sodom story demonstrates the judgmental wrath of God that is provoked by

---

[107]Rom. 1:26,27.

homosexuality, leading to temporal and eternal punishment; accordingly, Paul taught that God gives homosexuals over—abandons them—to dishonor, degradation, and depravity[108] and classifies them as "worthy of death."[109] The law of God strictly prohibits homosexuality in Israel as an abomination carrying the death penalty; accordingly, Paul declared that homosexuality is shameless error[110] which transgresses the ordinance of God and that its practitioners know that they deserve to die for their disobedience to God's will.[111]

In a sense, homosexuality is the cultural culmination of rebellion against God. It represents the "burning out" of man and his culture.[112] Paul described accompanying aspects of a culture that reaches this stage in verses 29–31.[113] The vices enumerated by Paul accompany the open practice of homosexuality and characterize a society in which homosexuality is practiced and tolerated. Therefore, homosexuality that is publicly accepted is symptomatic of a society under judgment, inwardly corrupted to the point of impending collapse. Paul the apostle regarded it as the most overt evidence of that degeneracy to which God in His wrath gave over the nations.

Consider, then, what God says in His infallible Word about homosexuality. It violates His holy law, representing a departure into abominable sin and shameless error. It is dishonorable, degraded, and depraved. These are not the judgments of some narrow-minded, uneducated, overzealous, modern-day crusader who is drunk with rhetoric. These are the judgments of the one only, living and true God, whose holiness, wisdom, and truth are flawless. Man, who was created by God in His own image, ought

---

[108]Rom. 1:24,26,28.
[109]Rom. 1:32.
[110]Rom. 1:27.
[111]Rom. 1:32.
[112]Cf. Rom. 1:27.
[113]"Being filled with" in Rom. 1:29 modifies "them" in Rom. 1:28, which is to say, the homosexuals of Rom. 1:26,27.

to reflect the purity of his Maker in thought, word, and deed. When men and women wander into homosexual perversion, thereby failing to conform to the righteousness of God, they dishonor themselves and degrade their own persons. That is why it is wrong for people to think that opposition to homosexuality is a violation of the homosexual's dignity as a person. It is precisely because of his dignity as a person that we must disapprove of homosexuality as unworthy of him as God's image.

It is untrue to the full extent of God's revealed will to reduce sexual ethics to questions of consent versus seduction, faithfulness versus promiscuity, etc. The form that one's sexual gratification takes is also a moral matter, and deviation from heterosexual monogamy brings the condemnation of God. This is contrary to the current attitude that says there is nothing intrinsically good or evil in any sexual act as such—that one's situation and attitude make his behavior right or wrong. As important as love is, the Bible will not support or condone the view that love can validate whatever expression sex takes (e.g., adultery, homosexuality, bestiality). Those who would defend homosexual desires and acts must reject an absolute standard for the form of one's sexual relations, but the Word of God presents just such an absolute standard. In the eyes of God the object of one's sexual gratification is not a matter of indifference, despite the protest of homosexuals against the normativity of heterosexuality. A certain irony is to be observed, however. Despite the moral relativism advocated by homosexuals with respect to the form of sexual relations, in other contexts they really want a positive value attributed to their own sexual preference! They want not only acceptance, but approval, demanding that everyone else respond as though homosexuality were perfectly respectable; they speak of homosexual relations as having virtue and beneficial consequences, they speak of themselves as "gay" (open and proud about their sexual orientation), and they give their organizations honorific names (e.g., Dignity). The Word of God refuses to render this kind of approval to the *homo*sexual form of sexual expression and behavior under any condition whatsoever.

It is the summit of evil when the sinner is so void of shame[114] that he is pleased with his vices and cherishes them.[115] Romans 1:32 indicates that the sins condemned are not the result of an irreversible and unavoidable inner "orientation," but are indulged in deliberately and encouraged in others. While modern interviews show homosexuals self-deceptively portraying their sexual attitudes and behavior as normal and desirable, Paul did not tolerate homosexuality, because in the eyes of God it is radical iniquity. Not only those who perform acts of homosexuality but also those who give approval to them have gravely offended the holy Creator.[116] Certainly disciples of Jesus Christ and the overseers in His Church should be far removed from any attitude and teaching that consents to homosexuality or effaces its sinful character. However, modern churchmen have instead learned to mirror the trends of the world. We would soberly conclude that modern society as well as the modern church are both dangerously close to divine retribution as they continue to tolerate and approve of homosexuality. "Gay liberation" is symptomatic of a culture abandoned by God to destruction and a church provoking the Lord with abomination.

---

[114]*Aschemosune*, Rom. 1:27.
[115]Rom. 1:32; cf. Prov. 2:14; Ezek. 16:25.
[116]Rom. 1:32.

3

The Act/Orientation
Distinction and Causes
of Homosexuality

It is necessary at this point to discuss certain recent claims that tend to qualify, if not dismiss the relevance of, the biblical data. According to a popular modern dogma the Bible cannot be thought to address what is understood as homosexuality today, for Scripture draws no distinction between the outward homosexual act and the inward homosexual orientation. It is precisely the latter (sexual inversion) that is taken as genuine homosexuality in current discussion. Moreover, the Bible does not seem to consider what causes the homosexual condition (inversion), and many today see ethical significance in such considerations. According to this theory the condition of inversion with all of its special problems was unknown in biblical times, and therefore Scripture's pronouncements must apply only to homosexual *acts* (or, others say, to homosexuality of the sort found when a constitutional heterosexual perverts what is natural to him).

Recent studies about homosexuality instruct the moralist to keep in mind the distinction between homosexual activity and the homosexual condition. The former may be transitory, situational, or traumatic behavior, and not necessarily the expression of the genuine homosexual condition as an inward orientation.

Thus to pass judgment on homosexual *practice* is not thereby to speak to the question of the inner homosexual *propensity*. There is a difference between external homosexual behavior and some inner factor, variously called a "predisposition, orientation, psychic condition, constitution, propensity," etc. This inner factor is described as a preferential attraction to the same sex, an emotional and physico-sexual propensity toward others of the same sex, a sexual desire directed toward gratification with the same sex, eroticism directed toward the same sex, a way of thinking and feeling, etc.

Because this psychological condition was allegedly unknown in the time of the Bible's composition, such inversion was not a subject discussed by its writers. However, modern science has recognized the existence of inversion, and the theologian must seriously consider what has now been learned through common grace and modify his conclusions about homosexuality accordingly. Most homosexuals are inverted either from the start or long before they understand what is happening within them. Whether a subconscious reaction, an involuntary tendency of the psyche, or an accident of personal development, the inner homosexual orientation is not something for which the individual is morally responsible. It is morally neutral, the ethical equivalent to being born lame or accidentally handicapped. Proponents of this viewpoint are divided over whether this inversion is a sickness or not, and whether overt acts following from it are likewise blameless or not.

What evaluation should be made of this distinction, upon which many writers insist? Perhaps the most important response is this: even granting the premise that the Bible never distinguishes between inversion and homosexual acts, the inference to be drawn may be just the opposite of that suggested. We are told that the Bible's condemnation of homosexuality pertains only to outward acts, since it does not isolate and discuss the inward orientation. However, one should draw the opposite conclusion:

if Scripture does not distinguish between orientation and act, the distinction is not morally relevant. Under the category of homosexuality, Scripture is to be understood as condemning both orientation and act, for there is no need in ethics to distinguish them.

Moreover, not only is their inference questionable, but the premise on which they rely is open to challenge also. They claim that inversion as a constitutional condition or psychic orientation was not recognized in biblical times, and that the Bible's teaching on homosexuality is therefore irrelevant in the light of recent discoveries. The Bible simply does not say anything about sexual orientation, which is the subject of modern discussion. Such a premise is faulty in at least two ways.

First, it seems to suppress the relevant fact that the primary Author of Scripture was God Himself, who is omniscient, and therefore does not need to have His revealed will in Scripture replaced or qualified by modern psychological guidance. Surely God knows man's inner life and the truth about his psyche. Man was formed by God, and all of man's life is lived in the environment of God's providential government of nature and history. But the fact remains that He does not distinguish between acceptable and unacceptable aspects of homosexuality in Scripture, and in Scripture is to be found everything sufficient for "training in righteousness, that the man of God may be fully equipped for every good work."[1]

It must not be forgotten that the law of God and the apostolic teaching both drew careful ethical distinctions and qualifications, indicating mitigating circumstances that affect one's judgment. However, unlike pagan writers who condoned or criticized homosexuality in different circumstances, Scripture allows no excuse but categorically condemns it. If it were crucial to our moral judgments that we distinguish between innocent inversion

---

[1] 2 Tim. 3:16,17.

and culpable homosexual acts, then certainly God would be aware of that distinction and bring it to light in His inspired Word for us. Without a doubt modern science can help us to understand our world better and thereby help us apply God's norms to life; however, science cannot establish ethical norms or alter those delivered by God the lawgiver. The utility of modern scientific research cannot be understood in such a way as to ignore the omniscience of God and the sufficiency of Scripture.

Second, the premise that the Bible does not address the issue of sexual orientation or propensity (inversion) is faulty in the most direct way. That the Bible shows no recognition of inner dispositions, firmly rooted character traits, or inherited propensities is a claim that is not sustained in reading. Scripture teaches that all men inherit a depraved, fleshly nature: a principle of sin operates in their members and captivates them,[2] the fleshly nature brings forth fruit unto death,[3] and it lusts against the Spirit so that men cannot do the things they would.[4] The flesh gives rise to certain forms of evil,[5] so that by nature men fulfill the desires of the flesh and mind.[6] It would be hard to understand such teachings apart from some notion of inner disposition and inherited orientation. The same holds for the doctrine that "out of the heart are the issues of life";[7] the Bible portrays man's heart as stiff, crooked, uncircumcised, deceitful, divided, hard, blind, and darkened.[8] Such metaphors demonstrate that biblical writers recognized an inner, spiritual depravity in men—a disinclination to good and a propensity for evil.

According to God's Word, man's psychological predisposition is calloused[9] and defiled;[10] men are enemies in their minds

---

[2]Rom. 7:23.
[3]Rom. 7:5.
[4]Gal. 5:17.
[5]Gal. 5:19.
[6]Eph. 2:3.
[7]Prov. 4:23.
[8]Deut. 10:16; Prov. 17:20; Jer. 9:26; 17:9; Hos. 10:2; Matt. 19:8; Eph. 4:18.
[9]Eph. 4:19.
[10]Titus 1:15.

against God and cannot be otherwise.[11] Therefore, we cannot deny that an inner, inherited, irresistible orientation of man's psyche was recognized in Scripture, and this condition was viewed precisely as the source of man's sinful activities. Men are drawn away by their own lusts, which conceive and bring forth sin.[12] As Jesus declared, "Out of the heart proceed evil thoughts, murders, adulteries, fornications, thefts, false witness, blasphemies."[13]

Thus there is an inner predisposition in all men that inescapably inclines them to evil and is the source of all their actual transgressions. Moreover, this *general* depraved nature common to men can be worked out into an habitual and besetting indulgence of *specific* sins; men can dwell upon and develop particular sins as forming a certain character. Reference to individual inner traits or personal dispositions is evident when the Bible speaks of men who lack self-control, are soon angry, have feet swift to shed blood, are presumptuous and self-willed, have eyes full of adultery that cannot cease from sin, are stubborn and obstinate.[14]

Consequently the notions were readily available by which the biblical writers could make reference to an inner propensity toward homosexuality; one cannot preclude the Scripture's ability to speak of inversion in some way, although not with the specific vocabulary of a recent science. If an alleged inner predisposition for homosexuality was relevant to drawing moral distinctions and making moral judgments, the Bible would not have been completely without ability to indicate so. Moreover, the fact is that God's revealed Word condemns homosexual *desire* itself, seeing it as sinful as well as homosexual *acts*.

To maintain that a person is not sinful for having homosexual attractions, feelings, or erotic orientation overlooks the clear bib-

---

[11]Rom. 8:7; Col. 1:21.
[12]James 1:14,15.
[13]Matt. 15:19.
[14]2 Tim. 3:3; Prov. 14:17; 16:32; Rom. 3:15; Isa. 59:7; 2 Pet. 2:10,14; Ezek. 2:4.

lical teaching that it is not only evil to do immoral acts, it is also evil to desire to do immoral acts: e.g., devising wicked plans or evil against your neighbor,[15] anger leading to violence,[16] malice,[17] envying dishonesty,[18] planning deceit,[19] loving false oaths,[20] coveting.[21] God's Word forbids sinful activities, but it equally forbids fleshly lusts or evil desires.[22] The classic passage in this regard is Matthew 5:27–29, where Jesus declares that everyone who looks on a woman to lust for her has already committed adultery in his heart. However, homosexual lust is in a sense even worse; while heterosexual drives are God-given, promote the cultural mandate, and are fulfilled within marriage,[23] homosexuality is always immoral in any context. Heterosexual desire is evil as lust (outside the marrige commitment), whereas homosexual desire is evil in itself (a perversion). In Romans 1 Paul does not restrict his censure to overt homosexual practices or "unseemly deeds." His condemnation extends specifically to the homosexuals being "inflamed with desire" for each other.[24] They are censured for having "impure lusts"[25] and "shameful passions."[26]

Therefore, it is plainly incorrect to hold that Scripture speaks only of homosexual acts and not of the homosexual desire and inclination. In forthright language Paul holds men and women morally responsible and under God's wrath for burning with homosexual desires, which he ethically describes as vile affections. The act/orientation distinction, then, does nothing to miti-

---

[15]Prov. 6:16–18; Zech. 7:10; 8:17.
[16]Gen. 4:7,8; Matt. 5:21,22.
[17]Eph. 4:31.
[18]Ps. 37:1,7.
[19]Amos 8:5.
[20]Zech. 8:17.
[21]Exod. 20:17.
[22]Rom. 13:14; Col. 3:5; 1 Pet. 2:11.
[23]1 Cor. 7:2–5; Prov. 5:18,19; S. of Sol. 7:1ff.; Heb. 13:4.
[24]Rom. 1:27.
[25]Rom. 1:24, where the word *akatharsia* literally pertains to refuse.
[26]Rom. 1:26.

gate the Bible's censure of homosexuality. We cannot agree with those who claim that Scripture knows nothing of sexual inversion, nor with their baseless judgment that a homosexual disposition is morally neutral.

Now in response to the preceding considerations, an adamant defender of the thesis that the homosexual has an involuntary psychological orientation that is unknown to the Bible and for which he is not morally responsible might contend that this inner condition cannot be identified with the desires condemned in the Bible. One might hold that what is taken as "inversion" today cannot be simply identified with homosexual affections or lusts, but is rather an inner, psychological disposition that lies behind and causes those desires (and acts, inevitably). The contention would be that a third factor must be admitted into the present discussion, a psychological orientation that is in addition to the inner homosexual passions and outer homosexual practices. And it is this third thing that some defend as morally neutral. The predisposition to homosexual attractions and behavior is not something for which the individual can be held responsible in ethical discussions.

What should be made of such a thesis? In a theological context it might mean that the depraved nature with which men are born is for some individuals specifically oriented to the sinful perversion of homosexuality. However, the Scripture does not support the idea that each person receives a sinful nature with a peculiar bent toward particular transgressions of God's will. Every man inherits a general depravity of heart, a fundamental disinclination to good, a pervasive misdirection, which affects every aspect of his person without discriminating emphases; there is a wholesale, general pollution operating in everything he is and does. Nevertheless, the ways in which individual sinners develop their depraved natures, the particular sins upon which they focus and around which their characters are formed, will differ from person to person. Thus everyone is born with a depraved sexual nature (i.e., a sinful predisposition that is expressed in the area of sex, as in all others); but individuals express this in various ways, be it lust, voyeurism, adultery, flirtations, exhibitionism, rape, frigidity, bestiality, sodomy, etc. No one is inherently *immune from* any one of these sins, and no one is specifically *impelled toward* any one of them on the basis of some distinctive complexion or form of that original sin that he individually inherits. Such an idea is foreign to the biblical doctrine of man.

However, even if it were somehow shown that this idea has biblical warrant, this fact would not lead in itself to the conclusion that the individual who has a distinctive sinful bent (say, toward homosexuality) in his inherited depraved nature is somehow less personally responsible for the corresponding desires and acts than for other sinful desires and acts. Adherents of the view in question have to show biblical support for the idea that the individual cannot be held specifically responsible for those particular sins that are *ingrained* in his depraved nature. Since everyone must recognize that original sin (however one views its characteristics and its manner of functioning) is itself sinful in character and something for which its inheritors are held personally culpable,[27] the notion that men are not specifically responsible for their particular *ingrained* sins can only mean mitigated culpability for the resultant desires and behavior proceeding from their distinctive depraved bent. But God's Word never offers such a mitigation of guilt for our lusts and practices; therefore the present theory contributes nothing to an ethical evaluation of homosexuality.

The secular version of the theory that homosexual orientation lies behind *both* desire and action asserts that something internal to certain men determines their homosexual attractions and actions. This "something" is labelled "a psychic condition, psychological disposition, physico-sexual orientation, or constitu-

---

[27]Rom. 5:12,15–19.

tional predisposition." Proponents of this view often insist that we distinguish between this orientation and overt acts of homosexuality. It is appropriate, then, to ask these proponents to draw the distinction—that is, to characterize or describe just what this *third thing* actually is that they want conceptually isolated and recognized. If the distinction is so very important, then someone ought to distinguish the underlying orientation for us. But this is precisely where proponents of the secular view turn out to be so sketchy in their discussions. It is as though they expect readers to be somehow automatically able to identify, understand, and use the mysterious notion of an "underlying psychological disposition." Just what is this supposed to be? Of course physicalists or materialists propounding this theory have particular trouble with analyzing psychological dispositions in general. Even apart from that, serious questions remain. Can a psychological disposition be identified apart from its manifestations? Can it be analyzed apart from necessary reference to desires and acts? Is this just another way to speak of homosexual desires and acts in summary fashion, while attributing independent substantival reality to this summary expression?

One possible account of dispositions is that they are conditional properties: e.g., to have a homosexual disposition means that *if* certain circumstances come about, *then* the person will manifest homosexual desires and/or practices. But then they are not causes at all and cannot be identified in isolation from actual manifestations of behavior. In that case the concept of dispositions becomes useless as an explanatory device, and the identification of a "disposition" involves circular reasoning.

Another account of dispositions is that they are actually properties of some definite state—akin to the structural qualities of physical objects—that is responsible for the person manifesting certain behavior. Since this view reduces what a person can be or do to what he is or is doing, we would expect that the character of the disposition actually would be manifested all the time. This is clearly contrary to the facts about homosexuals. No one holding this theory wishes to suggest that homosexuals are always having such desires and engagements. A further account of dispositions in the history of philosophy rests on an unpopular Aristotelian metaphysic of potentiality, wherein dispositional properties or predicates would not abide by the logical law of excluded middle (e.g., S is potentially having homosexual desire and is potentially not having such desires) and is extremely unclear.

Enough has been said to illustrate the point: dispositional analysis is an obscure question in philosophy to begin with. If psychologists who speak of "the homosexual disposition" are not referring to a conditional or actual property (with the attendant problems mentioned above), then what exactly are they referring to? What do they wish to distinguish for us? Moreover, what is it that allegedly has this disposition? Ordinarily we would think of the *person* having the disposition, but proponents of the present view often speak as though the disposition were attributable to some *element* of the person. Such an ambiguity allows for unwitting shifts in reference between some causal factor within the person, an *orientation*, and a characterization of the person himself. But a reference to *orientation* must either be taken as metaphorical shorthand, or it must be specified more exactly. Is it a physical or locatable thing that is thought to be constituted or oriented in a particular direction? If not, what is it? Finally, if persons are said to have a disposition to manifest homosexual desires and acts, can they also be said to have a *disposition* to have *that* disposition? Can they be disposed to be disposed to have homosexual desires? To put it basically, how can dispositions be distinguished from each other, and how do discrete dispositions relate to each other?

The relevant point of the above critique is simply this: If the distinction between homosexual orientation and acts is not a distinction between homosexual desires and overt acts, then those who insist upon the distinction must be thinking of some third thing apart from desires and acts—an alleged psychological disposition. However, those who so strenuously insist that this disposition must be distinguished have not distinguished or defined it clearly for us. And until they do, nothing can be made of their claim that it is morally neutral. Moreover, such a third thing apart from homosexual desires and acts is really inconsequential for ethics, in view of the fact that, whatever hidden factors may or may not be operative, Scripture holds the homosexual fully responsible for his desires ("impure lusts") as well as his overt activities ("unseemly deeds"). If a further third facet of the homosexual syndrome should be clarified conceptually and evidenced empirically, the Christian would still conclude that its nature cannot cancel culpability, for the teaching of God's infallible Word prevents drawing such an inference. Thus the existence of the alleged propensity would be beside the point ethically.

Let us now recapitulate the main points of our reply to the allegation that there is no distinction drawn in Scripture between outward homosexual acts and inward homosexual orientation (which was unknown at the time), and that therefore its condemnation must be restricted to homosexual practices (rather than propensities). First, even if the premise were accurate, the *inference* drawn would not be legitimate; we should rather conclude that the Bible addresses both act and orientation since it did not qualify its pronouncements, exonerating and setting some aspect of homosexuality apart from its condemnation. Second, the *premise* itself is taken in a way that conflicts with other theological truths, such as the omniscience of the primary Author of the Bible and sufficiency of Scripture for every judgment pertaining to the standards of righteousness. Third, the premise is straightforwardly *mistaken:* the ordinary metaphors and common-sense notions were available by which Scripture could have made reference to a homosexual disposition (understood as a characteristic inner lust), and in actual fact we find that God's Word explicitly censures homosexual desires and habits. Finally, the attempt to isolate the homosexual disposition as a different, third type of entity (apart from homosexual desires and acts)—in both its theological and secular versions—fails to demonstrate its distinct existence or its moral relevance.

This brings us to the question of what *causes* homosexuality. Differences of opinion have flourished here, and the "authorities" have been in conflict. Homosexuality has been attributed to a wide range of factors, from biological (e.g., one's body build) to psycho-social (e.g., oral regression). The only general fact to be acknowledged is that there is an utter absence of scientific agreement about homosexuality's cause and incidence. Many views that have been propounded have turned out to be unproven speculation—usually with implications that are contrary to Scripture. Although we will pay some attention to the debate over the cause of homosexuality, in the long run we must still ask what difference it makes in terms of morality. Even if we could identify with assurance the cause (or causes) of homosexuality, we would still have to confront the ethical question of its acceptability.

The two basic kinds of causes popularly put forward today to explain homosexuality are congenital and psychogenic. Is the homosexual *born* that way, or does he *learn* to be that way? For a long time the first was the central tenet of the permissivist stance regarding homosexuality, which claimed that glandular imbalance or some other biological factor was responsible for the homosexual's reactions. Thus he should be tolerated, as is anyone else who is born with a certain condition beyond his control. Some theologians, resting on such theories, reasoned that homosexuality was a part of creation or a result of the creation itself, and thus natural and futile to oppose. However, since this theory suggests that homosexuality is a physical abnormality or some form of sickness, it has lost popularity recently amidst public attempts to portray the homosexual condition as normal and dignified.

Meanwhile the congenital theories have lost nearly all semblances of scientific credibility. Empirical tests have failed completely to confirm any pattern of correlation between hormone levels and homosexual/heterosexual preferences; when male homosexuals were treated with estrogen, homosexual activity was found to slacken—but heterosexual drive was reduced as well. Attempts to redirect male homosexuality through injections of the male sex hormone have resulted simply in strengthening homosexual desire. Hormone experiments have not turned out to affect sexual orientation.

Another highly publicized conjecture was that homosexuality is a hereditary condition, but work done by recent geneticists has overwhelmingly refuted the idea. Not only has the view that homosexuality is a chromosomal anomaly been overthrown, but so also have many of the alleged "scientific" methods once used to bolster the view. Techniques developed for viewing all the chromosomes of a cell in connection with chromatin-sexing studies have found no abnormality relating to homosexuality. Research by sexologists has discovered that in studies of gender identity, non-genetic hermaphrodites are as free of homosexuality as individuals suffering from chromosomal disorders involving an absence in females or addition in males of the feminizing X chromosome (Turner's syndrome and Klinefelter's syndrome respectively). This evidence has definitively shown that homosexuality is a developmental condition and not constitutional.

Further, neuro-endocrine research has moved away from simple formulas and mechanical programming ideas for any behavior condition, including homosexuality. Genes and neuro-endocrine circuits are only a part of a creature's behavior system, and that portion is smaller and smaller in the higher species, reaching a minimal level for human beings, for whom adaptation and complex learning procedures assume immense explanatory significance. Biologically rooted concepts of homosexual "latency" have been recognized as begging the question by "explaining"

everything (both the absence and presence of homosexual manifestations) while clarifying nothing and lacking operational value
in hard science.

Finally, the last plank of the theory of homosexuality's biological normality has been removed by the most advanced ethologi-
cal studies, which have shown homosexuality to be uniquely
human. For years it was popular to think that many animals
engage in homosexual practices, but recently the evidence for
such a view has been found to rest on faulty observations, on
anthropomorphic misinterpretations, on confusions with heterosexual mating rituals and attempts to identify a sexual partner,
or on a truncated or special use of the term "homosexual." The
fact is that no mammal in its natural state seeks and prefers
same-sex sexual gratification (copulation, orgasm). This is found
uniquely among human homosexuals. Therefore, among many
contemporary scientists the theory that homosexuality is a biological condition (congenital, hereditary, or constitutional) is deemed
a theory without support, a conjecture demolished by hard empirical evidence.

We turn, then, to the psychogenic theories of homosexuality.
But first, let us pause to consider the turn of events in this century
relative to the homosexual polemic. Paul taught in the first century that homosexuality was a sinful preference. For this, Christ's
apostle was viewed as an ignorant bigot earlier in the twentieth
century. Psychologists said earlier in this century that homosexuality was an involuntary maladjustment, and thereby beyond
moral accountability. Current defenders of homosexuality want a
little of both. They now want to agree with Paul that homosexuality is a chosen pattern of desire and behavior, but they also want
to side with earlier psychologists that it is beyond objective moral
censure. Thus homosexuality would not be viewed as either an
involuntary affliction or an immoral option. Instead, it is set forth
as an innocent preference. Propounding this hybrid view suggests
that the discussion of homosexuality can now be carried on sim-

ply in an ethical framework, without much concern for its causes. However, even if psychogenic theories are becoming unpopular or only selectively utilized, we should still consider them on their own merits.

Among the adherents of the psychogenic theories one finds an emphasis on psychological (subconscious reactions) and environmental interaction. Some view homosexuality as a psychopathic condition, either emphasizing the constitutional component or stressing the experiential component. The difficulty with the former has already been discussed. The experiential component pertains to the emotional disturbance that has developed within the homosexual as he attempts to adjust to his various situations and social pressures. The difficulty with accepting the opinions of psychiatrists who view homosexuality as such an emotional disturbance is that they tend to have contact with only the individuals with personality conflicts and neurotic disorders, and not the "hidden" majority of homosexuals who have learned to get along with social and personal needs. Moreover, if the homosexual syndrome is taken as a neurosis or psychosis, it represents an individual's reaction to his society and vice versa; and it turns out that the very traits that such psychologists associate with homosexuality are also the emotional problems of individuals who identify with a persecuted minority in a society. That is, it is questionable whether those psychologists who view homosexuality as an emotional disturbance have been dealing particularly with same-sex orientation or rather with the person's response to society's harsh attitude (in this case, to homosexuality).

The practice and theorizing of many schools of psychology entail questionable assumptions such as the cogency of "subconscious" notions, the understanding of man that is utilized, the moral and evaluative presuppositions that are applied, the view that psychoanalysis brings a patient to recognize his operative beliefs rather than bringing him to new beliefs about himself, etc.

Further, psycho-social learning theories often operate with unclear, if not confused, notions of will and choice. It is not surprising, then, that the field is hopelessly divided today with respect to
the question of homosexuality. One would hope in vain if he
expected to receive some well-supported theory about the causes
of homosexuality from modern psychology. Psychologists strongly differ over questions as to whether homosexuality is abnor-
mal, is a sickness, is reversible, or is detrimental in itself to
being well adjusted. Thus those who argue that homosexuality is
constitutional or determined by complex and intricate psychological forces can legitimately be asked, just where is the evidence
that this is so?

There are plenty of conflicting theories, but little more than
speculation for each of them. To claim that one has "learned
from the sciences" that homosexuality is often a condition deeply
rooted in psychological aberrations for which the individual cannot be held responsible is a token of minimal familiarity with the
state of modern psychology, or it is hasty bravado. Moreover, it
must be recognized in the current discussion that modern psychology for the most part is concerned with how to handle
homosexuality, not specifically what and why it is.

Turning to the social side of psychogenic theories of homosexuality's causes, we can note first the recent work done by interdis-
ciplinary studies, making use of the research by ethologists into
the sexualized dominance-submission (dependence) expressions
of animals and men. It has been thought by some writers that
insights gained here would explain the psychodynamic core of
homosexuality, since the homosexual condition can be extensively correlated with social and interpersonal attitudes pertaining
to aggression, competition, dominance, humiliation, insecurity,
dependence, and submission. While studies in this area are often
quite imaginative (and one has the suspicion that subjective or
arbitrary explanatory patterns are imposed on the data), the fact
remains that even the more dependable work here is at best a

discussion of concomitant and contributing factors to the homosexual condition. Advanced scholars do not claim to be laying down the single key to homosexuality and adducing its cause, but only to be discerning connections with interpersonal relations and expressions.

Another popular tradition explains homosexuality in terms of the social environment of the family. It is suggested that factors in the relationship of the homosexual to his or her parents in early childhood led to the later condition of sexual inversion. For a boy this would mean a father who was absent or detached, one who was often hostile to the child or who minimized him in important ways, and/or a dominant mother (often frigid toward the father or other men) who tended to be overly intimate with the child and draw him into alliances with her against the father. While such a theory is popular today, and even fostered by some Christian writers, it can only be viewed as discussing a possible contributing factor and not a cause of homosexuality. As to its methodology, it can be questioned whether this explanation even says anything distinctive about homosexuality. Too many homosexuals have strong, loving fathers and non-dominating mothers, and too many heterosexuals have extremely maladjusted family environments, to think that any obvious correlation can be seen between homosexuality and early family relations.

Furthermore, some professionals have asked the telling question whether a person's homosexuality is the effect or the cause of what is later seen as the unfavorable parental atmosphere. Might not the father of a son who tended for other reasons to homosexuality become detached, disappointed, or hostile in response to a son he does not understand? "Homosexuality begins in the home" must be viewed as a dangerous and ambiguous platitude, even when used by Christian writers; it is certainly not supported by specific, solid evidence. Moreover, those advocating this position are usually less than clear on the question whether or not the homosexual (or his parents) is responsible for his behavior and response. For example, it has been said by some who attribute homosexuality to the home environment that society does not have the right to condemn an individual suffering from inappropriate choices resulting in homosexuality; yet the individual, according to the same authors, is responsible for learning new patterns of response and recognizing the sinfulness of his past patterns. One aspect of this outlook *establishes* what another aspect has *precluded*.

We must conclude that psychogenic theories of homosexuality are no more conclusive or persuasive than congenital theories. There is neither scriptural support nor solid medical evidence that homosexuality is a constitutional, involuntary, or irreversible condition. Moral responsibility for homosexuality has not been dissolved through scientific study.[28] The natural and human sciences have not, contrary to a widely publicized polemic, rendered any agreed-upon or individually substantiated verdict about the cause of homosexuality.

Perhaps in the future they will. But whether they do or not, the Christian will keep certain scriptural truths in mind. With reference to congenital theories, it must not be forgotten that God's Word teaches that homosexuality is not "natural" at all. Whatever physical factors may influence it, homosexuality cannot be viewed as biologically innate. It is artificial and learned contrary to what a man is by God's creation. Even in a fallen world with all of its distortions and miseries, Paul categorized homosexuality as "against nature"—as "improper," an "error," a fundamentally wrong way to live and use the human body. With reference to psychogenic theories, we would recognize that at base they make

---

[28]Because commitment to these theories is often quite strong (even though decided in advance of the evidence), it is not surprising that some theorists resist relinquishing them. Thus some now suggest that the cause of homosexuality is not *either* environment or heredity, but rather *both* in interrelation with each other. However, the discussion and analysis of such *interrelations* is a far from exact science (since interrelations are difficult to measure or confirm). Instead of offering hope of a scientific explanation of homosexuality, such a diehard suggestion appears simply as a doubly leaky bucket.

homosexuality out to be some form of learned behavior, a matter of one's reactions to social influences, environment, training, or exposure. This may or may not help some day to see which influences uniquely contribute to homosexual reactions, but the fact will remain that such learned behavior can be unlearned and altered.

One's personal reactions are crucial to psychogenic explanations of homosexuality, and Scripture always holds men accountable for how they react to their circumstances. No circumstance makes someone unavoidably sinful in his reactions, for there is always a way of escape pleasing to God.[29] All sin can be seen as having causes of one sort or another; no transgression arbitrarily "comes from out of the blue." However, these various causes, whatever they may be in individual cases, in no way remove a person's culpability before God. All sin is eventually traced by God to *our hearts*.[30] Whatever the external and internal circumstances, no one will be excused for his reactions if they transgress the revealed will of God.

Paul teaches that even the inward homosexual lust is sin,[31] and therefore in relevant respects it is engaged willfully and knowingly—not as an involuntary, ingrained, unavoidable orientation. Being sinful, homosexual desire is something for which men are held responsible by God. It may begin in various ways and under a variety of influences, but in the end it is nevertheless learned behavior which is abhorrent to the Lord. The homosexual's delight in and recommendation of his sexual perversion to others[32] indicates how willful is his participation in it. His homosexual deeds and desires are no more determined than are another man's heterosexual lusts and adultery. It is an unacceptable rationalization for a man to plead, "I am a constitutional

[29] 1 Cor. 10:13.
[30] Matt. 15:19.
[31] Rom. 1:24,26,27.
[32] Rom. 1:32.

adulterer, my lustful imagination is involuntary, and thus my misdeeds must be excused."

Scripture teaches us that our physical inclinations are to be subordinated to God's moral direction, not used as an excuse for transgressing it. And therefore the homosexual must channel his sexual drives in the right direction and exercise them, mentally and physically, under the limits set by God's will; toward his sinful and perverse condition he needs to assume the biblical attitude of repentance,[33] resistance[34] and redirection.[35] The common bisexuality among homosexuals (as well as the free adaptation of heterosexuals to homosexuality in certain circumstances, e.g., prisons) and actual results of proper pastoral counseling demonstrate that homosexuality is not an irreversible fixation. It is a willful orientation and adopted way of life that can be changed.

Of course homosexuality may not be a conscious and remembered choice any more than is heterosexuality. There may not have been a process of explicit deliberation, weighing the options, and coming to a decision in either case. But that does not make homosexuality or heterosexuality any less chosen, in the sense of a voluntary, willful, and personal preference. The occasional homosexual defense, "I can't help it," cannot be acceptable in light of the Word of God. Homosexuality is not a cross to be born, but a pattern of behavior to be thrown off with the old man and his lusts. Any Christian discussion of the act/orientation distinction or the cause of homosexuality that suggests that the inner desire is involuntary and perhaps irreversibly determined, and thus immune from responsibility, is contrary to the scriptural portrayal. Further, any such discussion that goes on to say that, although his inversion is unavoidable and permanently fixed in his disposition, nevertheless any outward expression of his

---

[33]Ezek. 18:30,31; Ps. 32:5; Luke 13:3,5.
[34]Eph. 6:10–12; 1 Pet. 5:8,9; James 4:7.
[35]1 Pet. 4:2–6; Eph. 2:2–10; 4:17–24; Col. 3:5–10.

homosexuality in overt acts is sinful and condemned, straddles the moral fence and is cruel to the sinner. God's Word portrays homosexual deeds *and desires* as willful, culpable, and able to be renounced through God's power. Such discussions as have been mentioned here offer the homosexual not redemption and release, but reinforcement or frustration.

The fact that homosexual desires and deeds are willful sins for which the person is morally responsible is overwhelmingly important if there is to be any hope in the Christian perspective on homosexuality. When responsibility for homosexuality is removed, hope for homosexuality is also destroyed. Authors who present homosexuality as an unchangeable inner domination by those drives or desires doom the sinner to despair. And such despair is unnecessary, unwarranted, untrue to Scripture. Because homosexuality is sinful, there is divinely guaranteed hope for its reversal. Christ came to die for sinners and to deliver them by His Spirit from their sins. Not only has our guilt been removed, but also our moral pollution is being set right.

Those who come to Christ are no longer slaves to sin and need no longer obey its lusts. In the power of the Savior's resurrection, effected by the Holy Spirit, sin no longer has dominion over believers.[36] They are now slaves to righteousness, resulting in sanctification of heart, mind, and bodily behavior. Because a person is a homosexual by will, and not by constitutional necessity, he can be changed and can reform his life. Having listed homosexuality among the things that exclude a person from God's kingdom, Paul says, "And some of you were these things"—but now they are washed, sanctified, and justified in the name of the Lord Jesus Christ and in the Spirit of God.[37] Therefore, on inspired and infallible grounds, the Christian can say that it *is* possible to turn from homosexuality and leave it behind;

---

[36]Rom. 6:1–22.
[37]1 Cor. 6:11.

it *can* take place—in the name of Christ and power of the Holy Spirit. What seems so impossible to men is possible with God. Moreover, He sanctifies men *wholly*, in both their desires and behavior.[38]

In summary, scholars with a naturalistic bias are in conflict over the homosexual's inner abnormality, cause, and cure. In the current discussion, divergent answers are guided by each scholar's particular presuppositions (e.g., his view of man, his criterion of normality, what he takes as warranting hope). This is true for the Christian as well. He has distinctive presuppositions derived from the revealed Word of God. They are the basis and guide for his view of homosexuality. With respect to the nature of man, the Christian sees him as a creature of God, given his definition and direction by the Creator, and thus always accountable to the Lord for the use of mind and body. With respect to a criterion, the Christian is firmly committed to the ethical standards of God's Word, and thereby sees homosexual desires and deeds as rebellion against the will of God. With respect to hope, the Christian looks to God's grace and power as able to change sinners and release homosexuals from the guilt and power of their willful perversion. These presuppositions, over against those fostered outside of commitment to God's Word, settle the issues pertaining to homosexuality's abnormality, cause, and cure for the Christian.

---

[38]1 Thess. 5:23; Gal. 5:24; 2 Cor. 7:1.

4

The Response of the Church: Hope for Homosexuals

The preceding sections of this study have elaborated the foundational truths by which a Christian can determine how the church and society should respond to homosexuals. The Scripture is taken as the inspired and infallible Word of God, to be understood according to appropriate principles of interpretation. The Christian ethic correctly and necessarily looks to the revealed law of God as an expression of His will for our lives. It must be concluded, on the basis of an examination of the creation account, the Sodom story, the law of God, and Romans 1, that homosexuality is unquestionably a sin in the sight of God. This censure cannot be evaded by drawing a distinction between homosexual orientation and homosexual acts, nor by searching for some cause for the homosexual condition. Scripture distinctly condemns homosexual desires, seeing the homosexual response as willful perversion. It sets forth the hope that men and women engaged in homosexuality (whether inverted lusts or external misdeeds) can be transformed by God's grace. Within the framework of these convictions it is possible to derive direction from God's Word as to how the Christian ought to relate to the homosexual in the life of the church and in the affairs of society.

An ever-increasing flow of rhetoric from unorthodox church-men maintains that homosexuality should be normalized and that the church should side with homosexuals as an oppressed minority. The propaganda can get quite heavy in this regard: "homosexuals are the scapegoats for fears felt by the majority in the church," "homosexuality is at base a heterosexual problem (inability to cope with one's own inverted feelings)," "a condemn-ing church and society are to blame for the promiscuity among homosexuals," "homosexual marriage should not be precluded simply because there is no possibility of conception," "it is a pitiful irony that the agency for proclaiming God's gracious and loving activity should behave so ungraciously and unlovingly toward people who simply have a different sexual orientation," and so on. These and similar charges are part of a campaign launched on the persuasive force of emotion rather than substan-tial exegesis, ethical reasoning, and good arguments. The aim of such accusations is, as many authors admit, to convince oppo-nents of homosexuality that *they* are in fact the guilty party, persecutors of healthy and brave people who want only the nor-mal rights of any human beings and acceptance in the church.

Many religious homosexuals maintain that they have learned to live with their desires and lifestyle apart from a bad conscience, that homosexuality is natural (perhaps God's answer to overpopu-lation), that it can express the love of God, and that homosexuals, therefore, should be accepted into the church as such and or-dained to the ministry when they feel so called. Since the church is thought to be primarily to blame for homosexual oppression, acceptance of homosexuals in the church would indeed have to be based on conversion—the conversion of heterosexuals away from their demeaning, categorizing, condemning attitudes to-ward those who are happy with their homosexual condition. As more than one writer has said, since the church must accept homosexuals (or else betray its mission) and not have a double standard in sexual ethics, it would be hypocritical to deny rites of marriage to them. Homosexual religious groups maintain that when it comes to church membership and ordination, their sexual orientation is God-given and need no more be changed than the color of a person's skin.

In contrast to such delusive personal opinions, Paul clearly and authoritatively placed homosexuals *outside* the kingdom of God. In 1 Corinthians 6:9,10 he wrote: "Do not be led astray; neither fornicators, nor idolaters, nor adulterers, *nor* homosexuals,[1] nor thieves, nor covetous, nor drunkards, nor revilers, nor swindlers, shall inherit the kingdom of God." Paul was very specific. Whereas all the other sins on this list are simply repeated from 1 Corinthians 5:9–11 (a similar catalogue of sins), the sins of sexual immorality are amplified into specific forms: fornication, adultery, homosexuality. And the latter category of sexual immorality is further detailed: Paul excluded from God's kingdom both *malakoi* and *arsenokoitai*. The former (literally meaning "soft, gentle," and in moral contexts "yielding, or remiss") refers to those who allow themselves to be homosexually misused, taking the passive role; the latter is in the masculine gender and is a compound from the words for "male" and "bed" (English transliteration, "coitus," from its Greek euphemism), thereby referring to men who have intercourse with men; it is analogous to the Old Testament reference to men who go to bed with ("lie with") other males— i.e., those who take the active role in a homosexual relation.

Paul introduced this list of those who are excluded from God's kingdom with the phrase, "do not be led astray." This seems to have been a technical expression used by Paul to charge Christians not to participate in the sins of pagans. It parallels Old Testament passages such as Leviticus 18:24–30, where God's people were instructed not to practice the abominations that characterized reprobate nations. "Do not be led astray" indicates

---

[1]Two Greek words are here rendered by the single English word, "homosexuals." Paul lists separately those who allow themselves to be homosexually abused and those who lie with men.

that it is precisely in such matters as this that men deceive themselves, rationalizing that God cannot mean His moral demands
seriously. This fundamental error is encountered increasingly
today in the form of ingenious but wayward defenses of
homosexuality.

The apostle of Christ, who represented and spoke for his Lord,
excluded homosexuals without qualification from God's kingdom
and thus from the church of Christ. Paul knew his detailed reference to sexual immorality would be interpreted as forbidding any
and all homosexual relations, regardless of the role one assumed,
the motivation and situation, or whether monogamous or promis-
cuous. And Paul's condemnation holds true even if a homosexual feels good about his homosexuality and proclaims he has no
sense of guilt. Hell will be populated with people who persuade
themselves of their innocence for the moment: "There is a way
which seems right to a man, but its end is the way of death."[2]
However the church must surely heed the words of Paul and
refuse to admit those whom God has excluded. The church can
no more accept unrepentant homosexuals than it can establish
congregations of practicing prostitutes, drunkards, swindlers, or
heathen idolators. The Lord of the church has discriminated
against such (along with all unrepentant sinners) in the fellowship
of the church.

This is not oppression; true concern for the homosexual on the
part of the church cannot be expressed when God's standards—
which were revealed for the good of man—are abandoned. It
would be only pseudo-compassion for churches to admit practicing, unrepentant homosexuals to membership, attempting to be
more humane than God Himself. The church ought not to be
the agent for undermining, ignoring, or disobeying the standards
laid down in God's infallible Word. The proclamation of this
Word is the church's unique commission.

---

[2]Prov. 14:12.

It must be concluded that practicing homosexuals should not be admitted to the church and, even more certainly, to its ordained offices. Rather the church must declare with Paul, "The body is not for immorality, but for the Lord."[3] The bodies of those who belong to Christ are members of Christ, temples of the Holy Spirit, and they are bought with a redemptive price; therefore, Christians must flee immorality and glorify God in their bodies.[4] Since homosexuals give manifest evidence that they are unsubmissive to these requirements and commit abominable sins against their own bodies,[5] they cannot make a credible profession of faith in the Savior without repentance from and repudiation of this sin.

To those supporters of homosexuality who argue, contrary to Paul's teaching in 1 Corinthians 6, that homosexuals deserve to be accepted as such into the church and that Paul's condemnation of them is not to be taken seriously today, we must point out Paul's further warning in 1 Corinthians 14:37,38. Anyone who does not recognize the things which Paul wrote as the Lord's commandment is himself not recognized by the Lord, nor is he a spiritual man.[6] By this the church can know the spirit of truth and the spirit of error: the one who genuinely knows God will listen to the apostles, and the one who is not from God will not listen.[7] As apostolic doctrine is a mark of the church of Christ, those modern assemblies that admit practicing homosexuals to membership and ordination jeopardize their Christian status—the very charge they level against churches that obey the apostolic instruction and "ungraciously" refuse admission to unrepentant homosexuals.

Defenders of homosexuality do not take Paul's words in 1 Corinthians 6:9,10 as we have, for three reasons. First, some ar-

---

[3] 1 Cor. 6:13.
[4] 1 Cor. 6:15–20.
[5] Cf. 1 Cor. 6:18.
[6] Cf. 1 Cor. 2:14,15.
[7] 1 John 4:6.

gue that the Greek words discussed above do not refer to homosexuality after all but have been translated inexactly through
scholarly preconceptions. According to them *malakoi* denotes
any form of immorality without a specific reference to homosexuality and *arsenokoitai* refers to excess in sexual behavior
and thus to male prostitution. However, such claims cannot
stand in the light of original sources, as nearly any commentary
on this passage that delves into original languages and background will demonstrate (e.g., Conzelmann). The evidence from
the second and sixth centuries A.D. that is adduced to support
revising our understanding of *arsenokoitai* can hardly cir-
cumscribe what Paul earlier meant in the first century. Moreover, it does nothing to prevent us from seeing a reference to
homosexuality, since the later instances deal with the corruption
of boys and anal intercourse—that is, precisely with homosexual
vices.

The idea that the plural form of the word must refer to sexual
excess and thus male prostitution is speculative at best and takes
its lead from an element of the word seen in another context.[8] It
overlooks the obvious construction of the word itself and is unnecessary to explain the plural, since Paul denotes groups of
individuals (plural) throughout the catalogue in which the word
is found. The understanding of *malakoi* is contextually clear
(being put in conjunction with *arsenokoitai*) and evidenced elsewhere in Greek literature (from as early as 245 B.C.).

A second reason for disputing the force of 1 Corinthians 6:9, 10
offered by supporters of homosexuality is that it conflicts with
evidence elsewhere in Scripture. We are told that, unlike the Old
Testament treatment of certain outcasts, the New Testament
church is supposed to accept eunuchs—that is, according to
Christ's word, anyone who does not marry and bear children.
The "eunuchs from birth" in Christ's statement are interpreted to

---

[8]Cf. Rom. 13:13, where the notion of excess is actually contributed by another word
altogether.

be constitutional homosexuals.[9] But this argument is even more speculative than the first one. There is no scriptural evidence that homosexuals were ever classified as eunuchs, and there is no good scientific reason to believe that homosexuality is a congenital and constitutional condition. Moreover, this interpretation contradicts the unity of Scripture, ignoring clear and contrary statements about homosexual abomination elsewhere in order to arrive at this fantastic understanding of select passages of Scripture. Finally, it must be noted that a eunuch is not merely someone who does not marry or have children; a eunuch is one who has no sexual relations at all, and thus a eunuch "for the sake of the kingdom"[10] is one who voluntarily abstains from sexual activity, having the gift of celibacy.[11] This is clearly not applicable to homosexuals.

Another passage said to conflict with the idea that 1 Corinthians 6:9, 10 excludes practicing homosexuals from the church is Galatians 3:28: ". . . there is neither male nor female; for you are all one in Christ Jesus." Here Paul allegedly taught that the moral ideal of love and justice set before the church utterly transcends all questions of sexual orientation. But this is reading into the passage what one wishes to find. Paul was dealing with sexual *identity*, not sexual *preference*. Furthermore, this oblique reference can hardly be used to undermine clear and detailed ethical instructions given by Paul in other places.

A third reason offered for rejecting Paul's exclusion of homosexuals from the church is that Paul was culture-bound and made obvious mistakes in moral judgment on other issues, such as slavery and woman's subordination. Lying behind such an argument is a faulty view of Scripture, its divine authorship, and its permanent moral relevance. Moreover, this polemic assumes wrongly that Paul taught unacceptable things regarding women

---

[9]Cf. Deut. 23:1; Isa. 56:2–8; Matt. 19:12; Acts 8:26–39.
[10]Matt. 19:12.
[11]Cf. 1 Cor. 7:7–9.

and slaves. Paul's endorsement of a slave's submission and of the biblical institution of slavery does nothing to justify the wicked oppression sometimes associated in our minds with the word "slavery." The scriptural teaching itself condemns those abuses that we customarily think of in relation to slavery. Forms of slavery may be morally acceptable according to God's Word, but the oppressive and lawless conception or use of that institution receives no support from God's Word. To think, then, that Paul made a moral mistake by endorsing slavery is as fallacious as thinking that, because some parents abuse their children, Paul was wrong to endorse parental authority at all. Likewise, it is a preconceived notion reflecting the modern cultural captivity of the gospel to think that a woman's subordination to her husband is contrary to Christian morality.

Therefore, we have not found any reasonable textual, contextual, or moral consideration that should dissuade us from the straightforward and apparent teaching of Paul in 1 Corinthians 6:9,10. Homosexuals ought not to be admitted to the fellowship of the church or ordained to ministerial office, for they are placed outside the bounds of God's kingdom altogether—along with all who transgress the law of God and rebel against His holy character.

We should be cautious regarding the constant refrain heard among evangelical writers that the primary response of the Christian church to homosexuals must be that of sympathy and not judgmental rejection, that we must love the sinner while hating his sin. Pity or sympathy is inappropriate if we are to think God's thoughts after Him and have our emotions transformed by the Word of truth. We cannot sympathize with those who commit what God deems abomination and perversion. God calls such people dogs, who are excluded from the New Jerusalem and are outside the kingdom of God. The sin was so heinous that in Israel it called for capital punishment. Accordingly the child of God must be repulsed and outraged at this vile behavior: "Therefore I esteem right all thy precepts concerning everything, I hate every false way."[12]

Sympathy is elicited when someone has been victimized or has fallen involuntarily into unhappy straits; we feel sorry for such people and respond with compassion. However, sympathy is out of place when it comes to capital crimes like murder, rape, kidnapping, or homosexuality. Many evangelicals seem to be deterred from taking seriously the judgment of God by an underlying belief that homosexuality is a constitutional condition that has victimized the homosexual like a disease, a condition for which he cannot be blamed. But this foundational attitude is mistaken, as is the conclusion that sympathy is the first attitude demanded of a Christian. Instead we ought to be shocked at such vile pollution and proclaim with certainty and clarity that God's holy judgment rests upon it. We must preach that the homosexual must feel sorry for his sin before God and be horrified by it, even as we preach the same attitude toward all sin. This is the Christian's primary response.

The only approach which does not destroy the integrity of Christian ethics or do injustice to the homosexual himself is the biblical message which teaches fundamentally that dreadful offenders of God's law are under His wrath and rejected from His kingdom—*unless* they are converted, repent of their sins, and cling to Christ in faith for salvation. In responding to the homosexual, the church must not forget this glorious qualification on God's wrath and must reflect the balance which is seen in "the kindness and severity of God."[13] It must manifest severe disapproval of homosexuality, but like the Redeemer it must *also* seek out the lost and show saving concern for them.

First Corinthians 6 explicitly and strongly condemns the homosexual; but it also brings the most blessed comfort and hope to the homosexual, because it unequivocally proclaims liberation

---

[12]Ps. 119:128.
[13]Rom. 11:22.

and salvation for him. Having said that homosexuals (along with other sinners) will not inherit the kingdom of God, Paul immediately added, "And some of you were such,"[14] but now are washed clean of it, sanctified from it, pardoned and declared righteous in spite of it. There *is* a way of escape for homosexuals.[15] There is a better hope than that offered by secular psychology, a confidence that one can be delivered from the guilt and power of homosexuality. Paul knew people whom God had saved from this abomination; their homosexuality was now in the past tense, a matter of their preconversion lifestyle. The gospel was the power of God unto salvation for them as well. The church should be encouraged by God's Word, then, to turn to current society with the good news, challenging the impotency of secular psychologists to help and change the homosexual. The church needs to be active in evangelizing the homosexual, taking the initiative for a constructive mission to the homosexual subculture of our day. The gospel of Christ applies as much to this form of sin and sexual misuse as to any other.

When men or women who have known this perversion embrace the gospel, the church can do nothing other than joyfully receive the repentant sinner. This reception belongs to all who turn from their sin, including the grossest of sexual offenders.[16] There is nothing in Scripture to suggest that certain immoral backgrounds should continue to keep a repentant believer from contact with the church; however perverse the habitual sins of a person may have been, they are forgivable. Those whom God has forgiven and accepted are not to be rejected by His people. The church may often have failed to carry into effect the equality of believers as fellow-sinners saved by grace, made fellow-citizens in God's household and joint-heirs with Christ. Though washed and forgiven, some sinners have yet been treated as somehow

---

[14]1 Cor. 6:11.
[15]1 Cor. 10:13; Heb. 2:17,18; 4:15,16; 2 Pet. 2:9.
[16]Cf. 1 Cor. 5:1–5,13; 2 Cor. 2:5–11.

untouchable, and this is to be deplored. The church is called to evangelize even the most unrighteous and ugly of sinners, rejoicing to receive them as brothers in the Lord upon their conversion. All repentant sinners must be extended the right hand of fellowship, whatever terrible and suspicion-engendering misdeeds may have preceded the saving work of God's grace in their lives. [17]

To be sure, homosexuals are not to be received into the church *as* homosexuals; the *past* tense (Greek: imperfect) in 1 Corinthians 6:11 must not be lost sight of. They had repented of their homosexuality and renounced it, and thus they had made a profession of faith that was credible. It is a cheap and powerless grace that some preach, neglecting to call men to repentance or to require ensuing sanctification. [18] And it is an imperfect perception of grace that leads some to say that we can accept the homosexual into the church just as long as he is not overtly practicing the sin, even though because of his constitutional condition he cannot help continuing to burn with homosexual passion or be afflicted with homosexual desires. Rather than so distorting God's grace, the church must show men the narrow gate, [19] calling on them to renounce their sinful conduct and trust the Savior. It must show men the power of their new resurrection lives, [20] explaining that there has been a transition from wrath to grace in their lives so that sin no longer has dominion over them. It must tell regenerated and converted homosexuals that God is not satisfied with sublimation of their homosexual desires and abstinence from overt acts; He requires a turning around from the inward desire, a renunciation of homosexual passion, and an attempt to correct it.

A homosexual's sanctification need not be complete to qualify for entrance to the church of Christ, but by God's grace he must

---

[17]Cf. Gal. 2:9; 1 Cor. 15:9.

[18]This is especially characteristic of some modern forms of unorthodoxy, which teach that everyone is redeemed already, being simultaneously under God's wrath and grace.

[19]Matt. 7:13,14.

[20]Rom. 6:1–22.

be resolved to avoid the sin completely—just as the sorcerer must renounce his magic, the heathen his idols, the murderer his violence. The point is that the same requirements are to be laid on the homosexual who becomes a Christian as are laid on every other converted sinner. The church cannot have a hypocritical double standard, whereby the sexual offender is expected to do either more or less than someone whose habitual sin is, say, selfishly ignoring the needs of the poor and the needs of his neighbor, or insisting on his own way and slandering those who do not comply, or a lack of self-control when it comes to traffic laws or eating, or any other offense to which the church so often turns a blind eye. We must shun a selective application of God's Word, seeing all converted sinners as in need of sanctification.[21] Paul does not single out homosexuals for special attention in the church, but classes them along with other kinds of sinners who without conversion could not inherit the kingdom of God. Recognition of that fact should go a long way toward correcting an often uneven hand or superior spirit in the church as other believers relate to converted homosexuals.

The church's two-fold responsibility toward the homosexual is this: (1) to proclaim God's just judgment on homosexual perversion, excluding the impenitent from the congregation; and (2) to announce the gospel as the power of God unto salvation, so that as repentant believers homosexuals may become fellow-members in the body of Christ. To this may be added a third obligation, to support and encourage them in a transformed lifestyle. The church must not only require a change of direction, but extend aid to the former homosexual in his Christian growth and in resisting temptation. The sin of homosexuality will not completely stop tempting the new convert any more than any other habitual sin immediately loses influence over a young believer. The problem will not necessarily disappear easily; it may take time, and it certainly will require pastoral counseling. The con-

---

[21]Acts 20:32; Heb. 12:14.

verted homosexual must not be expected to gain instant sanctification any more than the converted drunkard. That is why a lack of concern, a failure to uphold, an unhelpful and cold attitude toward the converted homosexual in the church is especially inexcusable. Christian fellowship can provide the climate needed for new moral direction and strengthening; it can help reshape a person's lifestyle, schedule, interests, and acquaintances. It can prevent loneliness and despair. It provides a shelter in temptation and an exhortation to keep sex in its proper place in life; it can make clear that new-found Christian liberty cannot be used as a pretense for the flesh.[22] Inverts must be assured that they *can* redirect their sexual desires, not by lengthy psycho-therapeutic treatment but by ethical confrontation and the means of grace. They must be encouraged that by God's Spirit they can indeed put their homosexuality behind them.

It will be especially necessary in this day to lay to rest the myth of constitutional homosexuality. When the Christian pastor or the new believer listens to this myth and takes it seriously, he is in danger of becoming deaf to the Bible's own teaching on the subject and substituting secular advice for the prescription of the Great Physician. In so doing he deprives the homosexual convert of needed hope. Moreover, the pastor and congregation of the church in which the converted homosexual seeks fellowship must make clear that his sanctification is not simply a matter of sublimating and being frustrated by his desires; such a half-way house is not where God intended to leave the homosexual when He delivered him from his sin. Since the homosexual has obviously not been given the gift of sexual abstinence, his restoration by God should eventually bring conformity to the creational order and a regaining of heterosexual desires. His final goal is God's ordained context and direction for sexual gratification— heterosexual marriage.[23]

In conclusion, the response of the church to the homosexual

---

[22]Gal. 5:13.
[23]1 Cor. 7:9.

must be that of Paul in Romans 12:1,2, urging them by the mercies of God to present their bodies as living and holy sacrifices to God, not conformed to this world but transformed by the renewing of their minds, so that they may prove the good, acceptable, and perfect will of God. To that end the church excludes unrepentant homosexuals and evangelizes them, showing the gospel to be the basis of forgiveness before God as well as the power of ethical renewal. When converted by God's grace, the homosexual must be wholeheartedly received by the church as a person for whom Christ died, and the church must exercise the same care and admonition toward him as for all repentant sinners. Encouraging the converted homosexual in his new life includes instruction in the means of grace, active Christian fellowship, and informed and practical pastoral counsel.

In short, the church must both express strong disapproval of homosexuality as a vile sin and engage in an effort to bring God's powerful and good news to bear on the lives of homosexuals. Here as always the Christian must strive in sincerity to speak Christ's full Word as from God, manifesting the knowledge of Him in every place, and thus being either an aroma from death to death or an aroma from life to life.[24]

---

[24]2 Cor. 2:14–17.

5

The Response of Society:
Homosexual Acts as Criminal

If we approach the Bible as the inspired and infallible Word of God and take biblical law as an expression of God's absolute moral will for man's behavior, we must conclude that homosexuality is a perverse sin. We turn now from a consideration of homosexuality as a sin to a consideration of it as a *crime*, from the personal to the public dimension, from the church's response to the state's. The leading question today is whether or not homosexuality should be deemed a civil right. Discussions of freedom and justice in society inevitably lead to a consideration of rights, for the concept of a right is basic to the concepts of freedom and justice. In the civil realm, to be free to do something is to have a right to it, and to perpetrate an injustice against someone is to violate his rights. Consequently, current polemics about freedom and justice for homosexuals are dealing with the issue of homosexuality as a civil right.

Before we can determine whether homosexuality is a civil right, we need to distinguish between different uses of the word *right*. "Right" can be used as an adjective, categorizing actions or attitudes as being either permissible, good, or obligatory; thus we say, "It would be right to tell him the truth." In this adjectival sense, right may apply to anything within the general realm of moral approval. However, right can also be used in a more restricted sense as a noun, in such statements as, "He has a right to read what he wants from the public library." When someone has a right, he has a claim on others; having a right implies some corresponding duty on the part of others.

The distinction between *being* right and *having* a right is illustrated by the statement, "It is right to contribute to the Red Cross, but the Red Cross does not have a right to contributions." This means that, although it is good and permissible to help the organization, the Red Cross does not have a claim upon such help (as though it were the duty of people to contribute). Furthermore, someone can have a right to do something without it being right to do it (e.g., "You have the right to overeat, but it is not right for you to do so.").

Such a distinction is possible because we recognize a difference between interpersonal obligations in a social context and wider obligations in a more general ethical context. In other words, there is a realm of private morality and immorality which is *apart from* the public claims and corresponding duties that the state enforces with civil sanctions. These two spheres cannot be strictly equated without making the state God. Therefore not all sins are crimes. For that reason, to say that homosexuality is not right (i.e., that it is sinful or immoral) is not to say it is not a right of people in society (i.e., that it is a crime). Therefore, Christians may hold on biblical grounds that homosexuality is *sinful* without automatically settling the question of whether homosexuality should be seen as criminal by the state. On the other hand, the distinction between being right and having a right does not prove that homosexuality is a civil right; after all, some sins are crimes as well. Not only do we deny that rape is right, we also deny that anyone has a right to rape.

So then, the question before us is not whether homosexuality is right, but whether people *have a right* to pursue homosexual relations. Recognizing that homosexuality is a sin, the Christian must go on to ask whether it is a civil right. But to answer that question requires distinguishing between different senses of "civil right"(or, between different duties laid upon others in accordance with a civil right). Sometimes by a civil right we mean a "freedom" right; in such cases a person is free to act without coercion, others have the duty of forbearance toward his decisions, and the state refrains from interfering with his behavior. Examples here would be the civil rights to free assembly, free speech, and private property.

In other contexts a civil right is a "benefit" right; in such cases a person has the right to receive something from others, who correspondingly have a duty to provide it and thereby satisfy the right. An example of this would be the alleged right of the disabled or elderly to welfare provisions.

Finally, civil rights are also taken in the sense of "nondiscrimination" rights; to possess such a right means that others are obligated not to regard adversely something about you when you desire employment, housing, education, public accommodations, etc. For instance, if a person has a civil right pertaining to skin color, nationality, or sex it means that these considerations must not be used to discriminate against him when it comes to extending services and opportunities.[1]

Unless we set apart the different senses of "civil rights," any discussion of homosexuality would quickly become confused. To maintain that homosexuality is a civil right might mean one of three things: (1) people have a right to pursue homosexual relations, and the state ought to refrain from bringing sanctions against that pursuit (i.e., homosexuality is a freedom right), or (2)

---

[1]Ironically, those who advocate "civil rights" in the second and third senses actually *reduce* "civil rights" in the first sense—namely, the individual citizen's personal liberty over against the organized power of the state. This not only shows how divergent the uses of the phrase are (and how unclear or ambiguous the polemical literature can thus be), but also how important it is to have an objective standard of crime (whereby individual freedom can be forcibly curtailed by civil officials).

people have a right to receive homosexual favors, and others have the duty to provide them (i.e., homosexuality is a benefit right), or (3) people have a right to be granted employment, housing, etc., without discrimination against their homosexuality, and others have a duty not to regard adversely sexual preference in such situations (i.e., homosexuality is a nondiscrimination right).

A civil right in the second sense is not the subject of current debate or the aim of defenders of homosexuality, and therefore we need not discuss it. What needs to be observed is the logical relation between the first and third meanings. To say that homosexuality is a nondiscrimination right clearly presupposes that homosexuality is also a freedom right, for it would be quite contradictory for the law to protect (in employment, housing, etc.) what it does not allow as a freedom (i.e., what it prohibits as a crime). If rape is a crime in the civil law, others have no duty to disregard the known sexual activities of a rapist when he applies for employment, housing, etc. If rape is not a freedom right, then it *cannot* be a nondiscrimination right either. Simply put, nondiscrimination presupposes noncriminality.

Thus nondiscriminatory laws in favor of homosexuality must presuppose that homosexuality ought not to be a crime with civil sanctions against it. If the Christian has grounds for the conclusion that homosexuality should be treated as a crime by the state, then he likewise has warrant for rejecting homosexuality as a civil right when it comes to employment, housing, etc. An attitude of nondiscrimination could be a duty only if homosexuality ought not be regarded as a crime within society.

To determine whether homosexuality is a civil right (in senses 1 *and* 3) we must ask whether it should be treated as a crime by the state. It should first be observed that no one can escape appealing to a definable moral principle or system when he answers the question of homosexuality as a civil right. One simply must not overlook the interdependence of civil law and ethics.

Consider, for example, the category of nondiscrimination rights. Christians have good reason to oppose making homosexuality such a right. While they may feel that discrimination based on involuntary factors such as heredity or physical conditions is immoral, they take a different attitude toward actions that are sinful (i.e., willful transgressions of God's law). In the case of some sins in some situations Christians will want to discriminate against those guilty of the sin (e.g., not wanting to hire a gambler as the company treasurer, a kidnapper as a playground superintendent, a drunkard as a bus driver, a prostitute as a teacher in a Christian school, a foul-mouthed person as the church pastor). In the case of homosexuality the Christian may especially wish to avoid placing those who publicize and promote their perversion in positions of influence, trying to prevent them from being role models in a school, from spreading distortions of the biblical view of marriage and the family, from tempting recent converts from homosexuality, etc. Understandably, the Christian will insist on discriminating against practicing homosexuals becoming pastors in their church, occupants of their rental house, or babysitters for their young people. Before God we are not only free, but morally obligated, to avoid social relations that specifically threaten to have sinful consequences.

Consequently, if homosexuality should become a nondiscrimination right in society, it would be at the cost of *depriving* Christians (and others) of their right to shun contact with moral perversion. Now if someone feels that Christians are wrong to feel such aversion to practicing homosexuals and that, therefore, they must be compelled by civil law to refrain from discrimination, he will be imposing his own moral principle or conviction on them. Moreover, he will create a favored class of people who gain an unfair position in the job market, for by making his sexual perversion known the homosexual is likely to be hired over other people, lest the employer be taken to court with a discrimination suit. He can justify taking Christian evangelists off the television

and radio if they condemn homosexuality. He can sponsor feder-
ally funded programs that will advance through the public
schools and libraries educational material exonerating homosexuality as an alternative lifestyle. He can present a different norm
and example than that of heterosexual monogamy to school children, thus directing them toward ungodly attitudes and ex-
perimentation. He can insist that television programs which present homosexuality as natural or desirable not be precluded from
public broadcast. He can utilize public money to make housing
available to homosexual couples.

In short, by imposing his moral perspective on others and
establishing homosexuality as a nondiscrimination right, such a
person effectively discriminates against Christians, depriving
them of their protections and freedoms, giving competitive ad-
vantage to homosexuals, and impairing the standards and training of the Christian home. There must be a moral warrant for
such discrimination, which makes it illegal for a Christian to
attempt to live consistently according to his moral standards in
social relations. On the other hand, if the Christian discriminates
against practicing homosexuals and deems their behavior criminal, then he will require (and offer) moral warrant for his attitude
and approach. In one way or another, then, someone's freedom
is going to be curtailed, and an appeal will have to be made to
personal moral convictions in the curtailing of that freedom.

It is important to remember this last point as we turn to the
question of whether homosexual behavior ought to be classified
as criminal. As previously noted, if homosexual relations are
criminal, then they can be neither a freedom right nor a nondiscrimination right, for no criminal can claim that others are obligated to tolerate him in the public display or advocacy of his
criminality. If the Christian has moral grounds for seeing
homosexual acts as crimes, then he has every right to urge the
state to forbid them and to discriminate against those who knowingly or admittedly commit such acts.

Of course, the fact that homosexuality is properly taken as a crime does not mean that homosexuals have no civil rights at all and can be treated in a shameful fashion. They would still retain, for example, the right to due process of law, to a fair and speedy trial, and to legal defense. Moreover, in asking whether homosexuality is properly a crime in order to see if it can be accounted as a civil right, the issue is not public lewdness, corruption of youth, or prostitution. These matters pertain equally to heterosexual vice and need no special attention here. Further, the civil issue of homosexuality has nothing to do with homosexual lust or internal attitudes of the heart (any more than heterosexual lust is a matter within the state's province), for the civil magistrate deals only with external, public behavior, with offenses discernible as overt acts.

The precise question is whether homosexual behavior in itself is criminal and thus should be denied specifically and separately the status of a civil right. In having civil statutes against homosexual acts, would society deny basic justice to the homosexual? Should a person's sexual preference be indifferent to the civil magistrate and should it be made a basic civil liberty?

To answer these questions we need to settle certain fundamental issues: What is the precise function of law within a society? What are the limits of legal coercion? What is the source of rights? Political life cannot be simply the skilled manipulation of power; it involves answers to evaluative and committal questions. It requires a moral stance (e.g., on the basis of obligation to the state, the prerogative to lay down legislation, the goal of legislation, the limits of state authority and legislation, and thus the rights of individuals). If a state had no moral base for its policies and statutes, then it could not differentiate between crime and punishment; that is, without a moral warrant for what it does, the state's punishment could be viewed as simply another crime of one group of individuals against others. For example, execution, imprisonment, and taxation would merely be euphemisms for murder, kidnapping, and stealing. The ethical basis for answering the preceding questions about the state must have a definite, circumscribed character; if it is arbitrary or inconsistent, then anything can be concluded from it.

The answer one offers to the question of whether homosexuality is a crime will be determined by his view of the state and its authority in legislation, which in turn will arise out of his specific, fundamental moral theory. Unbelievers have proven to be unable to justify their moral systems; either they have proposed authoritative principles that are so vague as to be irrelevant to specific questions or applicable in conflicting ways, or they have pronounced specific, relevant, moral judgments about a particular question without any authority by which to make their opinion binding on others. One does not have to read long in literature dealing with homosexuality as a crime or civil right before realizing how often proponents of particular answers leave unsubstantiated the ethical presuppositions and procedures that have led them to their present convictions.

Therefore the Christian should not be ashamed to use his biblical ethic to direct him in answering the question regarding homosexuality's civil status. Unbelievers must also appeal to their personal moral convictions in order to answer the question, and their underlying ethical systems do not withstand scrutiny with respect to both normative relevance and authority. Secular or humanistic views of ethics and the state either tend to find some justification for the state's authority but in principle lapse into totalitarianism, or they tend to find some justification for individual rights but in principle lapse into anarchy.

The Christian must realize how necessary it is to take a biblical approach to the state, civil legislation, and personal rights. To hesitate or refuse to do so is to resign oneself to the tensions, ambiguities, and arbitrariness of autonomous ethical schemes and political philosophies. If God has spoken with respect to the criminality of homosexuality, then the Christian need not—

indeed, must not—hesitate to bring God's Word to bear in the relevant area of society. The alternative is to capitulate to an alien ethic in answering the question—an ethic which has no justification, has severe internal discrepancies, rests on equivocal principles, and cannot protect us against totalitarianism or anarchy.

Christians have a mandate to promote a society characterized by justice. They recognize that God as Creator has moral authority over every creature and area of life; His will, reflecting His holiness, is an objective standard of right and wrong for all men in all ages. Accordingly Christians will want to repudiate a dichotomy between a sacred realm of grace (or religion) where God's revelation is followed and a secular realm of nature where autonomous standards of thought and behavior govern. All of life is religious. Thus the cultural mandate requires that every aspect of life be brought under the dominion of God and consecrated to His ends. Out of the heart are the issues of life (including political matters), and thus the renewed heart of the Christian will affect his approach to politics, even as it reorients his attitude toward all other areas of life. Christians do not consider the lordship of Jesus Christ as partial in scope; He always and everywhere exercises His kingly reign, requiring obedience of all men to God's standards. The earth is the Lord's and the fullness thereof, the world and they who dwell in it; all power and authority in heaven and earth have been given to the resurrected Messiah.[2]

On the basis of His unlimited authority and with the promise of His unlimited presence, Christ calls believers to the unlimited task of discipling the nations and teaching them to observe whatsoever He has commanded. Christians cannot escape their obligation to work for the transformation of every area of life, seeking foremost the kingdom of God and its righteousness, aiming to glorify God in everything they do.[3] Despite the reigning dogma of tolerance in modern culture, the biblically directed believer is

[2]Ps. 24:1; Matt. 28:18.
[3]Matt. 6:33; 1 Cor. 10:31.

committed to the transformation of every aspect of life and the subjection of all things to Christ.[4] His influence in the political arena must be like salt, light, and leaven—preserving from moral decay, scattering darkness, and permeating the whole with godly direction.[5]

The Christian must attempt to bring society into conformity with Christian standards for human interaction and with justice as defined by God. The values of believers in the area of political ethics are not set by a rebellious world bent on destruction, nor are they molded by secular humanists striving for increasing tolerance of public immorality. "The king gives stability to the land by justice."[6] "Evil men do not understand justice, but those who seek the Lord understand all things"[7]—that is, "those who keep the law."[8] After delivering the standards of God's law to Israel, Moses exclaimed: "What great nation is there that has statutes and judgments as righteous as this whole law which I am setting before you today?"[9]

It is God's Word that directs the believer to the true nature of justice and social rectitude. It is God's revealed standards that determine genuine equity, set just standards of crime, and establish human rights. God has sent forth His law and established His justice as a light for the peoples.[10] God's commandments are His people's wisdom in the sight of the nations.[11] It must certainly be the Christian's aim to see the law of the Lord as it is addressed to external civil affairs honored in national legislation, for "righteousness exalts a nation, but sin is a disgrace to any people."[12] The Bible pronounces woe on anyone who establishes a city by in-

---

[4]Acts 2:33–35; 1 Cor. 15:25; Col. 1:18; Matt. 28:19,20.
[5]Matt. 5:13–16; 13:33.
[6]Prov. 29:4.
[7]Prov. 28:5.
[8]Prov. 28:4.
[9]Deut. 4:8.
[10]Isa. 51:4.
[11]Deut. 4:6.
[12]Prov. 14:34.

iquity[13] because the throne is to be established by righteousness.[14]

From this necessary perspective the Christian can decide
whether homosexuality should be deemed a crime in society. In
the long run the criminality or freedom of homosexuality will
have to be decided within the framework of some ethical system.
The only question then is which system shall it be? In terms of
the character and defects of unbelieving systems, and in terms of
the Bible's own positive moral requirements as well as its evaluation of them, the believer has no choice but to settle the issue of
society's proper response to the homosexual on *scriptural*
grounds. Two basic kinds of argument have been raised to the
idea that Scripture should determine whether homosexuality is a
crime or a civil right. They can be roughly stipulated as the
"liberty ideal" and the "church/state polemic."

By the liberty ideal we mean a particular policy toward social
legislation (and Christian attitudes that are tied to it) that was
given classic expression by John Stuart Mill in the nineteenth
century and used as the basis of the Wolfendan Report's recommendation that homosexuality be decriminalized in Great Brit-
ain (1957). According to the liberty ideal a person has the right to
expect forbearance on the part of others from the use of coercion
or restraint against his activities unless those activities would
coerce or restrain the activities of someone else. Basically this
means that self-protection is the ground for interfering with the
freedoms of others through the agency of the state; if an activity
does not hurt anybody except the parties consenting to it, then
the state should refrain from legislation concerning that activity.

On this theory social law is enacted for the protection of society, crime being defined in terms of harmful effects on others.
Anything that interferes with a neighbor's safety or the exercise of

---

[13]Mic. 3:10; Hab. 2:12.
[14]Prov. 16:12. The obligation of any and all civil magistrates to rule in accord with the
law of God is further elaborated in my *Theonomy in Christian Ethics*, chs. 16–19,22.

his liberty should be prohibited, but victimless crimes or acts which hurt no one but the individuals willingly involved in them (e.g., acts between consenting adults in private) should be legally ignored. Each person should have the right to conduct his life in whatever way he pleases, as long as he does not thereby violate another's right to live his life as he pleases. Provided that one does not attempt to coerce others, prevent them from living according to their choices, or bring harm to them and or society, he ought to have the liberty to live according to his own choices. Accordingly, because homosexuality is a private and victimless form of behavior—not threatening a neighbor's safety or freedom—it should not be legislated against by the state. Sexual preference is a civil right indifferent to public morality in a pluralistic society. However regrettable one man may think another's choices are, that other man must be free to pursue his interests and activities without interference.

Two responses should be given to the liberty ideal. First, even if one were to endorse its basic principle (the criterion for deciding which acts are criminal), it would still be necessary for the Christian to maintain that homosexuality is a crime. Second, there are telling reasons why the basic principle cannot be accepted as a standard for social legislation over against the Scriptures. The liberty ideal does not lead to the conclusion that defenders of homosexuality envision, and the ideal is itself defective in many ways.

On the first point, it is shortsightedness that leads some social theorists to think that homosexuality has no ill effects on society. If homosexual relations are tolerated by civil law, thereby failing to witness against their abnormality and perversion and refusing to restrain their occurrence, the state allows a progressive degradation and permissiveness toward sexual matters. This is detrimental to the society's moral stability, the dignity of human beings, the attempts of people to live—and to raise their children to live—chaste lives, and the monogamous foundation that has been found crucial to all civilized societies.

To make homosexuality a civil right would open a Pandora's box of sexual immorality and thereby destroy the integrity of the family. We can reasonably expect that these effects would foster in turn a degraded view of man and his sexual nature (which in itself has significant implications for how people relate to each other in society). It would erode the familial foundation of the social structure, with its indispensable, intermediate disciplinary effect. People who are allowed to be unfaithful and perverse in sexual matters will hardly prove to be fit trustees of the rights of others—that is, to be faithful and upright regarding other moral standards or commitments.

Furthermore, there are social, psychological, and moral dangers posed when the law allows practicing homosexuals to be visible role models for others, especially children (and especially children of Christian parents). Teachers, law enforcement officers, neighbors, and others who make it known that they are unashamed homosexuals set forth what they deem as an "alternative life-style," but which God abhors as abomination. Thus even if the Christian should overlook the historical case of Sodom, the fact remains that social degeneracy will be the outcome of tolerating homosexual relations.[15]

The law of God is not an arbitrary code of rules with no relevance for personal and social well-being. The Lord revealed His law, as He Himself declares, for the good of man and his society;[16] obedience and disobedience of a culture will be expected to have resultant blessings and curses.[17] Therefore, the Christian should believe that there are good social reasons for God-given laws that confine sexual relations to monogamous,

---

[15]As Paul explains in Romans 1.
[16]Deut. 6:24; 10:13; 30:15,19,20; 32:46,47.
[17]Cf. Deut. 28.

heterosexual marriage. Even if we accepted the liberty ideal then, Christians would still oppose homosexuality as a civil right and want it recognized as a crime. After all, homosexuality is not an individual matter; it does bring harm to participants, families, and ultimately to society as a whole.

If the homosexual is encouraged by the law's tolerance of his behavior to accept his condition as normal and without ill effect, therefore declining to seek resources by which he can reverse his affections and renounce his activities, it may well be that "gay liberation" would be gained at the expense of a much deeper enslavement of the individual himself. Finally, it should be pointed out that civil laws against homosexuality should be encouraged, not because they will eliminate such behavior completely, but simply to insure that homosexual relations (when they exist) *will be*—as social proponents of decriminalizing homosexuality contend—totally private acts between genuinely consenting adults. Making homosexuality a crime will have the good effect of suppressing it and keeping its practice from public view and endorsement, even though homosexuals could still practice their perversion (as they say they wish) in private as consenting adults.

The Christian has every reason to apply the liberty ideal in such a way that homosexuality is the proper focus of civil legislation. But homosexuality's defenders will likely demur, saying that recognition of the above ill effects of homosexuality in society rests on commitment to the Christian moral system and biblical revelation, and therefore cannot be accepted in making social policy.

In response, a number of things should be said. First, rejection of the ill effects of homosexuality in society rests on a commitment to some other moral system than that of Scripture and likewise cannot be used in making social policy. If the liberty ideal prohibits using a distinct moral system to evaluate the consequences of social behavior, then it will be impossible to arrive at *any* social policy. If it requires using only those moral principles that are explicitly held by all men in common, then again a social policy cannot be derived—either because no explicit, universal agreement will be found,[18] or because the formal principle on which all men explicitly agree will be so vague or general that it is susceptible to conflicting applications.

Second, in answer to the objection to using a biblical outlook to anticipate and evaluate social consequences of homosexuality, it must be remarked that although it is the Christian who acknowledges these adverse consequences, what he acknowledges is nonetheless objectively true. Truth and assent are logically distinct, and thus it is futile to reject Christian conclusions in this area on the irrelevant ground that not everyone assents to those conclusions. If the liberty ideal requires us to consider only universally recognized consequences of some social behavior instead of the true consequences, again it would be impossible to form social policy.

Third, it is incorrect to think that only Christians are aware of those moral standards by which the effects of homosexuality are evaluated. The law of God by which the Christian judges these matters is known, although not explicitly acknowledged, by *all* men whether they are Christians or not, as Paul teaches in Romans 1:32 and 2:14,15. God's standards reflect His moral character, and every man is the image of God; moreover, every man lives in an environment through which God is continually, silently, clearly revealed. Therefore, men are totally without excuse for failing to submit to the truth about Him and His moral demands; they have sufficient provision to acknowledge the standards of God's law, but perversely refuse to do so.

It is incorrect to think that by going to God's Word in order to decide whether homosexuality is a crime, believers are trying to enforce a *distinctively Christian* ethic among unbelievers. The

---

[18]One wonders just how such a universal agreement could be confirmed empirically anyway.

fact that believers distinctively acknowledge the ethic as objectively valid due to God's work of redemption in their lives does not reduce their moral standards to mere private opinion that is subjectively derived. God is the Creator of all men, as well as the Redeemer of His elect; consequently, His moral standards are objectively valid and binding on His creature, man, whether or not men submit to them. The standards of genuine morality are universally valid and applicable and should not be disparaged as somehow true only for believers, as somehow uniquely Christian in content, as in some way sectarian. They are as absolute as the character of God, to whom all men are responsible.

Therefore, even granting the liberty ideal, homosexuality should be prohibited as a crime by the state. However, it should not go unnoticed that there are critical defects in the liberty ideal, defects that will turn out to require supplementing it by a specific moral system that exceeds the simple goal or standard of maximum social freedom. This is evident from the outset since the liberty ideal must be clarified, made consistent, and rendered applicable to homosexuality. Adherents of the liberty ideal must clarify what is meant by that "pain, harm, or injury" which no one has the right to cause in another. Newlyweds can cause their parents pain by moving to another part of the country where visiting will be very difficult; a person can cause his friend emotional harm by rebuking him; one merchant can cause another financial injury by opening a business in competition with him. Yet in none of these cases would we say that anyone's *rights* had been violated.

Adherents of the liberty ideal cannot go to the other extreme and define the injury that no one has the right to inflict on another as only physical violence, for threats and blackmail are just as much infringements on a person's freedom as assault. But threats generally cannot be taken as criminal violations of a person's freedom, for then facial expressions and personal gestures could amount to a transgression of civil rights as well. Hence the liberty ideal needs to clarify just exactly what kinds of injury or harm are not to be permitted against others if it is to be a workable criterion for limiting civil legislation. That requires it to be supplemented with a specific moral perspective that is not shared by all men. In that case the liberty ideal is not an independent alternative to biblical direction for the civil magistrate, nor does it end up permitting the extensive liberty that it originally promised.

Not only does the liberty ideal need to be clarified, its proponents need to be consistent in its application to social affairs. Without such consistency the theory is betrayed as insufficient or incorrect in practice. Adherents of the liberty ideal contend that the state should allow no coercion against a person in his free pursuit of desires, activities, plans, etc., unless that pursuit would hurt others; they customarily abhor the idea of civil interference in a person's life for his own good. Nevertheless, all of them fail to follow these principles consistently granting that there are exceptions (e.g., compulsory education, restrictions on the sale of drugs, protection against fraud, laws against cruelty to animals even though we eat them, prohibition of sexual acts with corpses, not admitting the consent of the victim as basis for a plea in charges of sado-masochism or deliberate murder). Moreover, adherents of the liberty ideal are usually unwilling to apply it to primitive cultures and children in civilized cultures.

We must recognize that there are certain standards of behavior that society ought to require to be observed, completely apart from considerations of personal freedom and consent. Here again is seen the veiled dependence on a specific moral system when the liberty ideal is put into operation, indicating that it cannot make freedom the sole criterion of social legislation.

The liberty ideal has been seen to be in need of clarification and consistency. Even if these things should be accomplished without appealing to some moral standard beyond that of freedom, the fact would remain that homosexuality is not an action

that affects only one individual. Homosexual relations cannot be
engaged in without involving the decisions, interests, and actions
of another. Does this amount to a criminal act against the other
person and a violation of his rights? Does it have consequences
that are detrimental to him and his best interests?

We have seen that the proponents of the liberty ideal will have
to decide what *types* of consequences should be taken into account in assessing criminality, and that such considerations will
take them beyond mere appeal to utilitarian assessments regarding freedom. However, in the present case, those who promote
the liberty ideal will say that such considerations, even if necessary, are beside the point because in legally sanctioned homosexual relations all participants would consent to such behavior—in
which case whatever the ill effects, they were not perpetrated
against their will.

However, such an appeal will need to be analyzed further if, as
most will intuitively recognize, a participant's consent is not
thought to condone certain crimes: e.g., virgin sacrifice in
satanist cults, drug overdose, consensual death in sado-
masochistic sexual relations, and "snuff films." Inevitably we
must recognize that moral men place high value on other things
besides freedom and consent: for instance, justice (rules against
unfair trials), security (laws against plotting to assassinate),
human life (laws against all willful murder), human dignity (laws
against seduction, defamation of character, public lewdness), and
interpersonal integrity (laws against manipulation of people
through false advertising and fraud). Furthermore, there are
some things so precious or important to a person that he will
often sacrifice his freedom because of them. The liberty ideal
cannot stand alone, but must be supplemented with a consideration of moral values that will lead to the imposition of particular
ethical standards on others who do not hold to them.

There are other defects in the liberty ideal that can be mentioned briefly. The ideal says that a man should be free to do what

he pleases unless he interferes with the freedom of others. We can appropriately ask what the moral grounds are for this qualification on a man's freedom. If liberty is of such high value as this theory purports, why should a man who is strong enough to get away with it (or even a man who thinks he is that strong) not ride roughshod over the liberties of others? Why should the state ever interfere with the actions of men? To believe that the state is morally unjustified in such interference is to turn men over to totalitarianism, where individual strongmen tyrannize others. To hold that the state is merely a voluntary association, in which case there should be competing governments (each with respective services, laws, courts, etc.) to which men freely submit or change their loyalties, is to reintroduce totalitarianism in the form of a warlord society. And thus the defense of freedom as the ideal for civil legislation or social relations ironically results in the loss of that very freedom. The tolerance of absolutely all opinions in a society will lead to relativism and to the destruction of the society as a body of men who relate by recognized laws to each other; for that reason the government requires its teachers to vow that they are not committed to its overthrow and passes laws against sedition.

Just where freedom should begin and be curtailed, then, is an unavoidable problem for the liberty ideal. And it cannot be resolved without applying the principles of an underlying moral system. In that case Christian morality cannot be precluded as defining certain actions as criminal and others as not. It especially cannot be precluded in light of the previously mentioned inability of unbelieving, autonomous systems to justify their ethic and validly apply it.

To take just one example, we may consider utilitarianism as a moral philosophy (i.e., the rightness of an act is assessed on the basis of its consequences, particularly on the basis of whether it will bring the greatest benefit to the greatest number). Overlooking many philosophical difficulties with this theory, let it simply

be noted that as a social theory utilitarianism leads to a view of
penal sanctions in society wherein one could justify the punishment of innocent parties. For instance, the execution of an innocent man could be warranted since it might maximize benefits
with minimal harm (e.g., it would put the town at peace since it
appears that the man who has been terrorizing women after dark
has been found and dealt with, it would increase respect and trust
for the police, it would deter others from contemplating similar
misdeeds). The point here is just that the acceptability of the
liberty ideal will have to be judged on the basis of a fundamental
ethical system, yet all secular systems of morality will be found
upon investigation to be critically deficient. The liberty ideal
must be evaluated as insufficient in itself and in need of a Christian foundation in order to be valid. Therefore it cannot undermine the conclusion that we should decide whether homosexuality is a crime on the basis of God's infallible Word.

The second major group of reasons why this conclusion is
rejected centers around a church/state polemic. Secular culture
today has misled many Christians into thinking that while they
may personally and ecclesiastically condemn homosexuality as a
sin, it is not the business of Christians to get unbelievers to accept
that evaluation in civil affairs. There is a difference between sin
and crime; while the Bible may define "sin," it is improper to
impose it upon a pluralistic culture as defining "crime" as well.
Since unbelievers have the religious freedom to decline being
Christians, they must also have the civil freedom to live contrary
to Christian standards on homosexuality. The state must not be
governed by the church, but kept separate from it. The state
cannot coerce people to live according to a distinctive Christian
ethic, for what some Christians consider evil on narrow scriptural
grounds ought not to be made a crime within an unbelieving state
apart from a demonstrable threat to public welfare or the common good. And thus it happens that morality as defined by God's
absolute law comes to be an internal, private matter of personal

holiness—without speaking to civil matters. On such spurious bases many modern churchmen advocate making homosexuality a civil right.

In response it must be noted that the doctrine of church/state separation has never been understood as the separation of the state from all ethical considerations, and such considerations are precisely what the law of God presents. Moreover, the separation of church and state—which was taught and guarded in both the Old and New Testaments—is a matter of the separation of two institutions and their respective functions. It does not entail a different objective moral authority behind both, nor does it indicate that God as the Creator cannot govern through His revealed law the behavior of all men as His creatures or that Christianity must be excluded from influence on the state.[19]

It is not a distinctively *Christian* ethic that the Scriptures require the state to enforce (as though unbelievers were compelled to take the Lord's Supper or tithe to a particular church), but simply God's universal and objectively valid moral standards. The state does not honor these moral standards in order to become an agency of the gospel or in order to deter all forms of sin, regardless of their criminal status. It simply submits to the moral law of God as an objective ethical standard by which the magistrate ought to pattern his rule, insofar as God's law is addressed to external, civil affairs. The state, just as the church, is "a minister of God," ordained by Him to serve His purpose, which in this case is the avenging of His wrath against those who violate His law.[20] The separation of church and state cannot be understood by the biblical Christian to undermine this revealed truth. If the general understanding of separation of church and state in present culture conflicts with the teaching of God's Word regarding the objective, moral requirements on the civil magistrate, then

---

[19]For further discussion of church and state in biblical perspective, see my *Theonomy in Christian Ethics*, ch. 20.

[20]Rom. 13:4.

the Christian knows which he must reject; the traditions of men cannot make void the Word of God.

God's law is to be promoted publicly[21] and not simply in our own private lives. Indeed, His law is to be advanced among kings and nations.[22] Christians are obliged to reprove the unfruitful works of darkness[23] with the light of God's law;[24] when they do not, they share in the guilt of sins committed through consent.[25] The moment believers become complacent toward the perverse sins of their society, they have begun to relax their grip on the sanctity of God's will. The social and civil values of believers are not set by the unbelieving world but by the revealed law of God. Not all sins are crimes, but those which God's Word defines as crimes (punishable by the civil magistrate) are to be treated as such in society. Therefore, it is not inappropriate but required of the believer to recognize the standard of God's law as indicating what sins should be punished as crimes by the civil magistrate.[26] The Christian, seeking to transform all areas of life by the Word of God, will teach that God never abdicates the throne of His sovereign righteousness in order to submit His laws to the sanction of a popular vote. He continues to demand justice in society—as defined by His law—even when men do not like its encroachment on their freedom.

When men assume a disdainful attitude toward the civil prohibitions set forth in God's law and try to evade His revealed insistence on civil intolerance toward certain acts, they must conclude that God judges with undue severity and that they themselves can be more loving or humane than the Creator. Not all of

---

[21]Ps. 51:13; 119:13.

[22]Prov. 16:12; Ps. 119:46,47; Matt. 28:19,20.

[23]Eph. 5:11.

[24]Isa. 51:4–8; Matt. 5:14–19.

[25]Ps. 50:18,21; e.g., Acts 8:1.

[26]What the specific penalty against homosexual behavior should be is not relevant to the present thesis; the point here is simply that homosexual acts are punishable and thus criminal. However, readers interested in the general question of biblical penology can pursue a study of it in ch. 21 of my *Theonomy in Christian Ethics*.

our moral convictions should be embodied in the civil law, but certain of them *demand* legal enforcement—even dictate "imposing one's views on others" when their behavior is deemed by God to be so gross as to require civil sanctions against it (e.g., murder, rape, kidnapping, stealing). Appeals to our "pluralistic" society are simply irrelevant in contexts such as these.

In terms of biblical revelation, it becomes apparent that social rectitude and justice, not universal tolerance or maximum personal freedom, are the end of government. Thus the moral gravity of an offense must be gauged according to what God's Word says about it; where God indicates that His minister, the civil magistrate, is to punish certain actions, then it can be legitimately considered a crime by the Christian.

Since homosexuality is a matter of public morality, it falls within the civil magistrate's province to deal with it.[27] He must "avenge God's wrath" against such "evildoers." Civil rulers have been ordained precisely for the purpose of enforcing justice in society, being God's deputies who express His vengeance[28] against those who transgress God's law.[29] This is the pervasive outlook of God's Word. In *both* Old and New Testaments, and with respect to *both* Jewish and Gentile rulers, Scripture teaches that God sovereignly appoints and removes rulers, who bear religious titles and as His deputies are avengers of His wrath. Therefore, magistrates must deter evil but honor the good, which entails ruling according to God's law and being subject to punishment for lawlessness. The kings and judges of the earth are commanded to serve the Lord with fear and to exercise discernment.[30] God judges in the midst of rulers, condemning those who rule unrighteously.

Because their thrones are established on righteousness, it is an

---

[27]Rom. 13:1–4.
[28]Rom. 13:4; cf. 12:19.
[29]Cf. Rom. 13:10.
[30]Ps. 2:10–12.
[31]Ps. 82:1,2.

abomination for kings to commit wickedness[32] rather than ruling in the fear of God.[33] When Paul wants to describe the evil ruler *par excellence*, the one who will undergo God's judicial wrath, he characterizes him as "the man of *lawlessness*";[34] the Beast substitutes his own humanistic law for God's law.[35] If God is to hold civil rulers accountable to Him for their government, what standard of judgment will He use if not His own revealed law? Can there be sin where there is no law? To make the magistrate accountable only to "common prudence" is to dissolve ethics into inclination and sociology; moreover, it opens the door to untold tyranny and cruelty in the ambiguous name of common prudence. The Christian ethic is one of revealed law from God. Thus either the magistrate has ethical obligations (in which case he is responsible to God's revealed law) or he does not (which is terrifying, not to say unscriptural, in its implications).

Therefore, we conclude that the law of God as it is addressed to the civil magistrate properly indicates what actions should be taken as criminal in the state. The civil magistrate is to be God's minister, avenging His wrath against evildoers, who violate His law. Therefore, since the law of God clearly requires that those who lie with men as they would with women should be punished by the state,[36] it is not consistent with a biblical view of man or society to endorse legislation that decriminalizes homosexuality today.

Bible believers have God-given rights to influence the state in all lawful ways to maintain or establish criminal laws against homosexual behavior. Christians may accordingly vote against proposed legislation that would classify homosexual acts as a civil right and would prohibit discrimination against practicing homosexuals. The pluralism of American society provides no

---

[32]Prov. 16:12; cf. v. 10.
[33]2 Sam. 23:3,4.
[34]2 Thess. 2:3.
[35]Rev. 13:16–18; cf. 14:1,12 with Deut. 6:8.
[36]Lev. 20:13.

justification for repealing laws against sexual perversion or endorsing laws that would punish the failure to extend services and opportunities to practitioners of such perversion. Criminal legislation against homosexual acts or more general social intolerance toward those who engage in them are "discrimination" against homosexuals only in the sense that laws prohibiting fraud discriminate against liars and social intolerance toward those who embezzle discriminates against thieves. The only question is whether homosexuality is to be classified along with crimes such as these. If it is, then Christians ought to campaign and vote in such a way that the attitude of their general (pluralistic) culture and of the official laws of the state will be one of disapproval toward homosexual behavior.

God's Word does not view homosexual activity as anyone's civil right; rather, the magistrate has a God-given right to interfere in the behavior of men at this point, restraining their homosexual behavior along with the crimes of murder, kidnapping, perjury, etc.[37] One of the purposes for which God's law was enacted, says Paul, was to restrain public immorality. It is "lawfully used"[38] when applied to restraining such misdeeds as homosexuality.[39] And one God-ordained avenue for such public restraint of evildoing is the civil magistrate.[40] Accordingly, the Christian will view homosexuality not only as a sin, but also as a crime. If homosexuality is properly taken as a crime, it cannot be thought of as a civil right in any sense. Others have no corresponding duty to tolerate such behavior because the civil magistrate is charged by God with punishing it. Nor are others obligated not to discriminate against those who commit such misdeeds. Rather, people have the right to avoid criminal associations in employment, housing, etc.

---

[37] 1 Tim. 1:8–10.
[38] 1 Tim. 1:8.
[39] 1 Tim. 1:10, *arsenokoitai*.
[40] Rom. 13:3,4.

All civil law will be legislated morality, in some sense infring-
ing on someone's freedom. The civil law does not aim to regen-
erate men but simply to restrain their outward behavior. Such
laws are necessary to a social order, establishing the limits of
liberty and the public standards to which all members of the
community must conform. God has infallibly decreed that the
prohibition on homosexual relations is one standard and limit on
human activity that is to be recognized in the social order and
enforced by the state, thereby guarding the creation ordinance of
heterosexual marriage.

6

Conclusion

A general moral consensus among people in the church and in society at large once rendered the subject of homosexuality almost too shameful to mention in public and certainly placed a consideration of such perversion as a "right" out of the question. But that was a former day, and the consensus has disintegrated. Now homosexuality is openly and boldly advocated by vocal factions within the church and society, campaigning to have us accept it as respectable or, at least, indifferent. The discussion and ethical evaluation of homosexuality—which is bound to have far-reaching consequences in home, church, and state—cannot help but generate distress, disagreement, tension, and confusion in the midst of our current ideological and social conflict.

However, Christian ethics and social policy are not dictated by majority opinion and popular sentiment. Despite the outspoken campaign of homosexuals to be viewed as normal and treated like everyone else, Christians must remain true to their distinctives as determined by the written Word of God. This not only calls for resisting ungodly conclusions, it requires the integrity not to be drawn into, or led astray by, the muddled reasoning, emotional appeals, question-begging inferences, irrelevant grounds, and inconsistent thinking that all too readily dominate current polemics for and against homosexuality. Our decisions must be made on scriptural principle. And our principled conclusions, hopefully supported by cogent and coherent reflection, must be maintained even in the face of unpopularity.

Christ's disciple will also strive to avoid falling into fallacious, either-or options. He need not choose *either* to show gospel compassion *or* social and moral condemnation. Rather, not only will he determine to preach God's gracious way of redemptive deliverance—the message of forgiveness; he must also stand firm for the specific norms of behavior as revealed in the Bible—the message of divine requirement and restraint. Indeed, the former will presuppose the latter. Furthermore, believers should be careful to observe important distinctions within the host of questions about homosexuality confronting us today. To inquire into developmental factors regarding homosexuality is not to settle anything with respect to its moral evaluation and responsibility. It is one thing to speak about overt homosexual acts, another thing to discuss underlying attraction to such acts; the fact that we can distinguish between these two does not entail a different ethical judgment about each. To answer the question, "Is homosexuality immoral?" is not to answer all the questions about the church's relation to those guilty of this sin. There is a difference between an admitted, practicing homosexual and a repentant homosexual. There is a difference between the way the state and the church should respond to both. The list of relevant distinctions could continue.

In the study that has been presented here we have been led to conclude that homosexuality itself—both in practice and desire—is a grave sin in the sight of the Lord. The quality of interpersonal feeling, commitment, respect, etc., which may or may not exist between homosexual partners (be it beautiful or ugly in particular cases) does not affect this evaluation in the least. Homosexuality is not made wrong by a bad attitude, nor made right by a good attitude toward the object of one's homosexual desire or behavior. Homosexuality is not morally neutral. It is itself an abomination, totally apart from its circumstances. We are all sinners, to be sure; but that does not disqualify us from recognizing and deploring, nor does it compel us to rationalize what the Bible clearly rejects as contrary to the will of God. Thus we must insist that it is an extremely mistaken and eternally damaging opinion to maintain that any Christian's growth toward mature Christian living could include remaining open to or attaining full sexual partnership with a person of the same sex. More fundamentally, because no person is at liberty in the sight of God to engage in a willful pattern of unrestricted sin of any kind in any area of life, it is firmly required by the Bible that membership (and thereby ordination) in the church be denied in principle to unrepentant homosexuals—just as much as to unrepentant adulterers, liars, racists, etc.

This conclusion is not mitigated by consideration of the cultural background and alleged scientific ignorance of the biblical writers, nor is it qualified or refuted by modern studies in psychology, medicine, and sociology. God does not—and has not been found to—contradict His clear message in Scripture by information revealed through nature, history, or any realm of creation. God's written Word sets forth the male-female distinction as part of God's design for mankind, requiring that sexual relations be within the boundaries of heterosexual monogamy. Considerations of one's psychological "constitution" and of sociological statistics are not in a position to contradict the declaration of Scripture that homosexual desires and acts are perversions. The homosexual is morally responsible for his attraction to, and sexual relations with, members of the same sex. This is true regardless of how one thinks about the ambiguous question of whether homosexuality is consciously chosen, and regardless of what light science might in the future shed on the psycho-social forces inclining people toward homosexuality. (I refer to "future" light because it is manifest to any responsible observer that the sciences have no stable, clear, strongly evidenced position that is advanced by a consensus of "experts" at the present time.) If future findings in psychology, medicine, or sociology are strictly irrelevant to altering the moral evaluation of homosexuality, then it stands to reason that the "failure" of the biblical writers in the past to know the results of these findings is inconsequential.

In the long run, those who wish to disagree with Scripture's judgment that homosexuality itself is immoral will need to assume a perspective on Scripture that is contrary to its own self-witness. Divergent ethical opinions on homosexuality held by professing Christians will nearly always trace back to different views of scriptural authority. Some view the Bible as written by men whose opinions were *materially* conditioned by their time and place (and not simply conditioned with reference to language and manner of expression); accordingly, the teachings of the Bible may be set aside, refuted, or qualified by modern scholarship. Such a view does not take the words of Scripture to be the very words of God, who speaks with unquestionable authority and truth. Others approach the question of homosexuality being willing to abide by what the Bible, as the infallible and fully inspired Word of God, says, and to see the work of various fields of endeavor in the light of Scripture's primary teaching. Some approach the Bible as having an evolutionary or inconsistent perspective on moral matters, thus leading some to pit the Old Testament commandments against the New Testament attitude and leading others to adjudicate conflicting claims by some further ethical consideration or standard. On the other hand, some view the Bible's ethic as uniform and permanently binding, from Old through New Testament, and thereby view us as obliged to draw our personal and social conclusions in ethics on the basis of every stroke of God's revealed Word.

Thus the issues facing us today are deeper than the difficult question of homosexuality. The authority of God's Word and the normativity of His law are also at stake. The continual pressure of public propaganda tends to wear down the believer's resistance to homosexuality on the basis of the Word of God, thereby subtly undermining his view of Scripture as well. The drift away from the Bible's authoritative teaching on the subject of homosexuality, whether in personal, ecclesiastical, or social dimensions, is manifestly toward concession. With renewed conviction and firmness the church of Christ must pronounce the genuine and distinctive Word of God regarding homosexuality. It is perversion and sin, degrades man as God's image, and deserves eternal wrath. Continued indulgence disqualifies a person from membership in the body of Christ and ordination to Christian service.

Just as this conclusion is not mitigated by empirical science or critical study of Scripture, it likewise does not warrant unmitigated rejection of the homosexual. The church cannot be true to its mission on earth and turn away from evangelizing homosexuals, accepting them, when they repent, into the fellowship of believers, and nurturing their growth in sanctification. In this regard homosexuality is not a separate category of sin, as though it were unforgivable or placed the offender in a perpetually untouchable condition in the eyes of the church. The concern of the gospel is for the unrighteous—without distinction. This precludes any attitude of moral superiority among sinners saved by grace. This commits one to mutual love and edification with all of God's people, whatever their background. It calls us all to a common cup of the Lord. As such, the gospel leaves no room for a loathing fear of the homosexual (popularly labeled "homophobia" today) or a contempt that prevents bringing him the hope of God's gracious deliverance.

The social question, however, is whether overt homosexual behavior (known through legal due process) should be a crime in the eyes of the state, and whether it is permissible for people to discriminate against admitted homosexuals in opportunities and services which would otherwise be extended to them. Do homosexuals have a civil right to their sexual attractions and relations, such that the state should not have laws against homosexual acts but rather laws prohibiting discrimination by employees, landlords, etc. against avowed homosexuals. The unfair suffering of homosexuals in the past (e.g., entrapment, harrassment, prejudiced trials) is not relevant to answering such a question; nor does a negative answer to the question justify making homosexuals suffer in any conceivable way. The question is simply whether homosexuality is a civil right in some sense. It cannot be settled on the basis of what might be *perceived* by any particular group as beneficial or harmful to the parties involved and affected, but rather on the basis of what God's unqualified moral order requires. If homosexual acts are not restrained by civil law, then the community at large will be "harmed," some say. But if homosexual acts are declared a crime, then sanctions imposed on the homosexual will "harm" him, others say. Some argue that allowing an avowed homosexual to teach children will be "harmful" to these students. Yet others reason that denying a job to the homosexual will cause him "harm." Which "harm" will be morally decisive (what kind of harm, and whose)?

The question of civil rights for homosexuals cannot be answered on the basis of past sufferings (of either homosexuals or their opponents) or perceived benefit and harm (to homosexuals or their social community). The issue is really over the function of civil law, its moral foundation, and the place of the state. The Christian has biblical grounds for particular attitudes toward each of these matters. The state is ordained by God to serve as His minister, restraining and punishing those who violate His commandments as they are addressed to civil relations.

Governing agencies are not warranted in protecting citizens from just any immorality or supposed moral danger. Sin and crime must be distinguished—objectively, not by majority opinion. The majority may well determine what things will in practice be deemed a crime within a particular society, but the majority opinion is not the objective standard of what in fact ought to be taken as criminal. The Christian's attitude is not determined by a social barometer but by the Word of God. Therein we can discern both the limits of state interference in moral issues (e.g., it has no authority to punish overeating) as well as its positive requirements (e.g., it must avenge God's wrath against theft, murder, etc.). Therefore, laws which would punish convicted homosexuals and defend the individual's right to deprive admitted homosexuals of social association, opportunity, or services would not be based simply on the fact that homosexuality is immoral. Otherwise such laws and rights to discriminate would apply to all men, for all have sinned (and in terrible ways). A further, specific warrant is required for taking homosexual sin (in overt acts) as criminal or deserving of social discrimination.

It has been argued above that the standard by which followers of Christ decide which sins must also be taken as crimes is *not* the liberty ideal. It is ambiguous, inconsistent, and untrue to say that a community can restrain (through criminal law or the right to discriminate) certain practices only if their exercise injures a significant group of people in some important way, as discerned by empirical evidence accepted by the majority of citizens. Rather, the objective standard of crime is God's revealed law. As seen in the previous study, God holds magistrates accountable to Him, requiring that they rule according to the justice revealed in His Word. The standards of social morality laid down in Scripture are as valid today and to be promoted by the believer as are the standards of private morality. Because God's law requires the state to restrain homosexual activity, there is moral justification for the Christian to support criminal laws against homosexuality and to deny social opportunities and services to those who knowingly practice homosexual acts.

The fact that, according to the objective moral standard of God's Word, homosexual acts are criminal does not mean, of course, that every society will in practice obey God's directive.

The point being made in the preceding study is that states that are willing to do so have moral justification in making homosexual behavior subject to civil sanction, and that Christians ought to oppose the decriminalization of homosexuality in modern society. Moreover, and more to the point in our immediate situation, the state ought not to forbid social discrimination against homosexuals in employment, housing, services, and accommodations, and Christians have full justification in confidently working against laws that prohibit discrimination based on admitted homosexual behavior.

The conclusion that the state is right to restrain overt homosexual activity and that discrimination against practicing homosexuals is morally permissible surely does not mean that homosexual activity will cease or become impossible. It simply means that such criminal activity cannot be broadcast, flaunted, or promoted. Legal or social restraints against homosexuality should have the effect of driving it into secrecy and away from public influence. Laws prohibiting homosexual behavior and social discrimination against admitted homosexuals guarantee that homosexual acts will genuinely be in *private* between consenting adults. The same is true of any number of other crimes: civil law restrains them, and yet they are committed in private. The fact that some criminal activity can be cautiously pursued and thereby be secret enough to escape civil sanctions does not alter the criminal character of such acts or the appropriateness of civil laws prohibiting them. Their public display and pursuit is thereby suppressed.

In concluding that homosexuality was a perverse sin and that unrepentant homosexuals could not be admitted to the church, we found it necessary to go further and explain that this does not give license for unqualified rejection of the homosexual, whereby evangelistic concern and Christian fellowship to the repentant are withheld. Likewise, in the area of civil morality, the fact that homosexuality ought to be viewed as a crime and citizens ought to have the right to discriminate against those who practice it does not give license for the state to restrain it in an unqualified fashion. Methods of detection and conviction and the treatment given the accused by law enforcement officials, if deemed unjust in other contexts, are also unjust when it comes to homosexuals. Consequently the use of entrapment techniques, invasion of privacy, harrassment, persecution campaigns (wherein only one class of offenders is singled out for pursuit and punishment), and whatever else is against just treatment of citizens cannot be condoned on the basis that homosexuality is not a civil right. In a lawful and fair society even those accused of criminal activity do not forfeit all civil rights. The Christian should insist on that, just as much as he maintains that homosexual acts are not to be sanctioned by civil law.

Any definable, clearcut position taken on the issue of homosexuality today will prove inflammatory; yet attempts to strike a middle course will become unhelpful equivocations. To be sure, unbiblical extremes must be avoided. Not all homosexuals can be classified as seductive corruptors of little children. On the other hand, opposition to laws that prohibit discrimination against homosexuals is not to be aligned with the Inquisition or the Nazi movement. Such polarizations violate the ninth commandment. Still, a precise, biblically grounded position must be assumed, even should it prove unpopular. The only genuine balance available to the believer—one which will avoid extremes but not escape controversy—is the infallible teaching of God's written Word. Today as always this is the light upon our path that can keep us from stumbling.

Therefore, this study has taught that the Christian must have a *twofold response* to homosexuality. He must work for righteousness in society, petitioning the civil magistrate to avenge God's wrath against evildoers, and he must work for the salvation of individual homosexuals, rebuking sin and offering the restorative grace of God in the gospel. Evangelism is not inconsistent with the social endorsement of God's law, for the Great Commission demands *both*.[1]

Thus the Christian's attitude toward the homosexual should parallel his attitude toward other criminals. While not wanting them to be free to practice their sins without equitable punishment, the Christian still must have the compassion to evangelize those who face far worse punishment before the throne of God. The Christian should be concerned about purging social evil from his land, as well as to bring all who will repent to faith in Jesus Christ. To pit one duty against the other is to fail to be subject to what the whole Bible has to say on homosexuality. Homosexuality is not a civil right. We are not obligated to respect its practice and refrain from intervening against those who engage in it. But neither is homosexuality a bar to entering the kingdom of God through conversion.

The Christian directed by God's Word must avoid both an unholy *sympathy* for the homosexual and an unholy *hatred* for the homosexual. To tolerate homosexuality in the spirit of gay liberation or the gay church is disrespectful to God's righteous demands. To treat the criminal homosexual as a subject for rehabilitation rather than retribution is to dismiss the restraining function of God's revealed law and thus to abandon society to the vile condition described by Paul. However, to consign the homosexual a place outside of evangelistic concern, to loathe this sin as somehow worse than one's own, or to discriminate against converted homosexuals who wish to participate in the worship and fellowship of the church is unrighteous indignation and pride. It may be easier to take an extreme attitude either of self-righteous hostility or of unrighteous sympathy, but neither extreme is pleasing to our Lord. To please Him our attitude must reflect His—in all His purity and grace.

---

[1]Matt. 28:18–20.

Bibliographies for Further Research

HOMOSEXUALITY IN RELIGIOUS PERSPECTIVE

Bailey, D. S. *Homosexuality and the Western Christian Tradition.* New York: Longmans, Green, and Co., 1955.

Blair, R. *An Evangelical Look at Homosexuality.* New York: Evangelicals Concerned, 1972.

———. *Consultation on Theology and the Homosexual.* San Francisco: Council on Religion and the Homosexual, 1967.

———. *CRH: 1964–68, The Council on Religion and the Homosexual.* San Francisco: Council on Religion and the Homosexual, 1968.

Davidson, A., pseud. *The Returns of Love.* Downers Grove, IL: InterVarsity Press, 1970.

Joint Committee on Homosexuality. *Report of the Diocesan Committee on Homosexuality.* San Francisco: Episcopal Diocese of California, 1966.

Jones, H. K. *Toward a Christian Understanding of the Homosexual.* New York: Association Press, 1966.

McNeill, J. J. *The Church and the Homosexual.* Mission, KS: Sheed, Andrews & McMeel, 1976.

Oberholtzer, W. D., ed. *Is Gay Good? Ethics, Theology, and Homosexuality.* Philadelphia: Westminster Press, 1971.

Pittenger, N. *Time for Consent? A Christian's Approach to Homosexuality.* London: SCM Press, Ltd., 1967.

Tobin, W. J. *Homosexuality and Marriage.* ——— Catholic Book Agency, 1964.

Treese, R. L. *Homosexuality: A Contemporary View of the Biblical Perspective.*
   San Francisco: Glide Urban Center, 1966.
The United Presbyterian Church U.S.A., Office of Church and Society of the
   Board of Christian Education. "What About Homosexuality?" *Social Pro-
   gress*, November–December, 1967.
Wilkerson, D. *New Hope for Homosexuals.* New York: Teen Challenge, 1964.
Wood, R. *Christ and the Homosexual.* New York: Vantage Press, 1960.

SEX IN BIBLICAL, CHRISTIAN, OR MORAL
PERSPECTIVE

Atkinson, R. *Sexual Morality.* New York: Hutchinson, 1965.
Babbage, S. B. *Sex and Sanity: A Christian View of Sexual Morality.* Philadel-
   phia: Westminster Press, 1967.
Barnhouse, R. T. *Male and Female: Christian Approaches to Sexuality.* New
   York: The Seabury Press, 1976.
Henry, C., ed. *Baker's Dictionary of Christian Ethics.* Grand Rapids: Baker
   Book House, 1973.
Brun, J. E. *The New Morality.* Philadelphia: Westminster Press, _____.
Buckley, M. *Morality and the Homosexual.* London: Sands, 1960.
Cole, W. G. *Sex and Love in the Bible.* New York: Association Press, 1959.
_____. *Sex in Christianity and Psychoanalysis.* New York: Oxford University
   Press, 1966.
DeKruijf, T. C. *The Bible on Sexuality.* De Pere, WI: St. Norbert's Abbey
   Press, 1966.
Ditzion, S. *Marriage, Morals and Sex in America.* New York: Bookman As-
   sociates, 1953.
Epstein, L. *Sex Laws and Customs in Judaism.* New York: Bloch Publications,
   1948.
Hastings Encyclopedia of Religion and Ethics. Edinburgh: T. & T. Clark, 1908.
Heron, A., ed. *Towards a Quaker View of Sex.* London: Friends Home Service
   Committee, 1963; rev. ed. 1964.
Kardiner, A. *Sex and Morality.* Boston: Routledge & Kegan Paul, 1955.
MacQuarrie, J., ed. *A Dictionary of Christian Ethics.* Philadelphia: Westmins-
   ter Press, 1967.
O'Neil, R. and Donovan, M. *Sexuality and Moral Responsibility.* Washington,
   D.C.: Catholic University Press, _____.
Patai, R. *Sex and Family in the Bible and the Middle East.* Garden City, NY:
   Doubleday & Co., 1959.

Pittenger, N. *Making Sexuality Human*. Philadelphia: Pilgrim Press, 1970.

Smedes, L. B. *Sex for Christians: The Limits and Liberties of Sexual Living*. Grand Rapids: Wm. B. Eerdmans Publishing Company, 1976.

Taylor, M., ed. *Sex: Thoughts for Contemporary Christians*. Garden City, NY: Doubleday & Co., 1972.

Thielicke, H. *The Ethics of Sex*. Grand Rapids: Baker Book House, 1975.

VARIOUS RESPONSES IN THE CHURCH TO HOMOSEXUALITY

Adams, C. F. *Some Phases of Sexual Morality and Church Discipline in Colonial New England*. _____, MA: Wilson and Son, 1891.

Adams, J. E. *Christian Counselor's Manual*. Grand Rapids: Baker Book House, 1973.

Bishops' Committee on Pastoral Research and Practice. National Conference of Catholic Bishops, 1973.

Gearhart, S. & Johnson, W. R., eds. *Loving Woman/Loving Men: Gay Liberation in the Church*. San Francisco: Glide Publications, 1974.

Kuhn, D. *The Church and the Homosexual: A Report on a Consultation*. San Francisco: Council on Religion and the Homosexual, 1965.

Lucas, Donald S., ed., *The Homosexual and the Church*. San Francisco: Mattachine Society, 1966.

LEGAL PERSPECTIVE AND CIVIL LIBERATION

Altman, D. *Homosexual Oppression and Liberation*. New York: E. P. Dutton & Co., 1971.

Bahnsen, G. L. *Theonomy in Christian Ethics*. Nutley, NJ: Craig Press, 1977.

Bailey, D. S. *Sexual Offenders and Social Punishment*. Westminster _____: Church Information Board, 1956.

The Challenge and Progress of Homosexual Law Reform. San Francisco: Council on Religion and the Homosexual, 1968.

Churchmen Speak Out on Homosexual Law Reform. San Francisco: Council on Religion and the Homosexual, 1967.

Devlin, P. *The Enforcement of Morals*. London: Oxford University Press, 1959.

Gebhard, P. et. al. *Sex Offenders*. New York: Harper & Row, 1967.

Grey, Antony, *Christian Society and the Homosexual*. Oxford: Manchester College, 1966.

Keeling, M. *Morals in a Free Society.* Naperville, IL: SCM, 1967.

Masters, R. E. L. *The Homosexual Revolution.* New York: Julian Press, 1962.

Ploscowe, M. *Sex and the Law.* Englewood Cliffs, NJ: Prentice-Hall, 1951.

Report on the Roman Catholic Advisory Committee on Prostitution and Homosexual Offences and the Existing Law. London: Roman Catholic Church in England, 1956. (Reprinted in *Dublin Review,* 230 [Summer, 1956], 57–65.)

Rushdoony, R. J. *Institutes of Biblical Law.* Nutley, NJ: Presbyterian & Reformed Publishing Co., 1973.

———. The Politics of Pornography. New Rochelle, NY: Arlington House, 1974.

Salvatorian Justice and Peace Commission: Gay Minority Task Force. 1972.

Schur, E. M. *Crimes Without Victims.* Englewood Cliffs, NJ: Prentice-Hall, 1965.

Slovovenko, R. *Sexual Behavior and the Law.* Springfield, IL: C. C. Thomas, 1965.

Shackleton, Edward R., *Religion and the Law.* Ridbeugh, Kilbirnie, Ayreshire, Ireland: E. R. Shackleton, 1966.

Temple, W. *Christianity and the Social Order.* Oxford: Penguin Books, 1942.

"The Consenting Adult Homosexual and the Law." *UCLA Law Review,* XIII (March, 1966).

United Church of Christ, Council for Social Action, "Civil Liberties and Homosexuality: An Issue in Christian Responsibility." *Social Action* (Dec., 1967).

The Wolfenden Report . . . On Homosexual Offences and Prostitution. Briarcliff Manor, NY: Stein and Day, 1963.

HISTORICAL PERSPECTIVE

Abbott, S. & Love, B. *Sappho Was a Right-On Woman.* Briarcliff Manor, NY: Stein & Day, 1972.

Cory, D. W. *The Homosexual in America.* New York: Greenberg, 1951.

Flaceliere, R. *Love in Ancient Greece.* New York: Crown, 1962.

Hunt, M. *The Natural History of Love.* New York: Alfred A. Knopf, 1959.

Karlen, A. *Sexuality and Homosexuality.* New York: Norton, 1972.

Laver, J. *Manners and Morals in the Age of Optimism.* New York: Harper & Row, 1966.

Lewinsohn, R. *A History of Sexual Customs.* Greenwich, CT: Fawcett Books, 1964.

Licht, H., pseud. *Sexual Life in Ancient Greece*. New York: Barnes and Noble, 1963.

Tarnowsky, B. *Pederasty in Europe*. N. Hollywood: Brandon House, 1967.

Taylor, G. R. *Sex in History*. New York: Vanguard, 1954.

Toon, M. *The Philosophy of Sex According to St. Thomas Aquinas*. Washington, D.C.: Catholic University of America Press, 1954.

SOCIOLOGICAL AND GENERAL TREATMENTS

Becker, H. S., ed. *The Other Side: Perspectives in Deviance*. New York: Free Press, 1964.

Berg, C. & Allen, C. *The Problem of Homosexuality*. Secaucus, NJ: Citadel Press, 1958.

Cappon, D. *Toward an Understanding of Homosexuality*. Englewood Cliffs, NJ: Prentice-Hall, 1965.

Carpenter, E. *The Intermediate Sex*. Reading, MA: Allen and Unwin, 1908.

Comfort, A. *Sex in Society*. Secaucus, NJ: Citadel Press, 1966.

Cory, D. W. & LeRoy, J. *The Homosexual and His Society*. Secaucus, NJ: Citadel Press, 1963.

Cory, D. W., ed. *Homosexuality: A Cross Cultural Approach*. New York: Julian Press, 1966.

Gide, A. *Corydon*. New York: Farrar, Straus, 1950.

Goffman, E. *Stigma*. Englewood Cliffs, NJ: Prentice-Hall, 1963.

Gagnon, J. H. & Simon, W., eds. *Sexual Deviance*. New York: Harper & Row, 1967.

Gross, A. A. *Strangers in Our Midst: Problems of the Homosexual in American Society*. Washington, D.C.: Public Affairs Press, 1962.

Hause, R. *The Homosexual Society*. _____ British Home Ministry, 1962.

Hoffman, M. *The Gay World*. New York: Basic Books, 1968.

Kennedy, E. C. *The New Sexuality: Myths, Fables, and Hangups*. Garden City, NY: Doubleday & Co., 1972.

Kinsey, A. C. et. al., *Sexual Behavior in the Human Male*. Philadelphia: W. B. Saunders, 1948.

_____. *Sexual Behavior in the Human Female*. Philadelphia: W. B. Saunders, 1953.

Kohn-Behrens, C. *Eros at Bay*. New York: G. P. Putnam's Sons, 1962.

Krich, A. M., ed. *The Homosexuals*. Secaucus, NJ: Citadel Press, 1964.

McCaffrey, J., ed. *The Homosexual Dialectic*. Englewood Cliffs, NJ: Prentice-Hall, 1972.

Ruitenbeek, H., ed. *The Problem of Homosexuality in Modern Society.* New York: E. P. Dutton & Co., 1963.

Shofield, M. *Sociological Aspects of Homosexuality.* Boston: Little, Brown and Co., 1965.

Secor, N. A. *The Same Sex.* Philadelphia: Pilgrim Press, 1969.

Storr, A. *Sexual Deviation.* Oxford: Penguin Books, 1964.

Symonds, J. A. *Studies in Sexual Inversion.* New York: Medical Press, 1964.

Tripp, C. A. *The Homosexual Matrix.* New York: McGraw-Hill Book Co., 1975.

Walker, K. & Fletcher, P. *Sex and Society.* Oxford: Penguin Books, 1955.

Weinberg, G. *Society and the Healthy Homosexual.* Garden City, NY: Doubleday & Co., 1972.

Weinberg, M. S. & Williams, C. J. *Male Homosexuals: Their Problems and Adaptations.* Oxford: Penguin Books, 1974.

Weltge, R., ed. *The Same Sex: An Appraisal of Homosexuality.* Philadelphia: Pilgrim Press, 1969.

West, D. J. *Homosexuality,* 2nd ed. Oxford: Penguin Books, 1968.

Westwood, G. *Society and the Homosexual.* New York: Dutton, 1953.

PSYCHOLOGICAL AND MEDICAL

Allen, C. *Homosexuality: Its Nature, Causation, and Treatment.* London: Staples Press, 1958.

Beach, F. A., ed. *Sex and Behavior.* New York: John Wiley & Sons, 1965.

Beigel, H., ed. *Advances in Sex Research.* New York: Hoeber Medical Div., 1963.

Bergler, E. *Homosexuality: Disease or Way of Life?* New York: Collier Books, 1967.

Bieber, I., et. al. *Homosexuality: A Psychoanalytic Study.* New York: Vintage, 1965.

Churchill, W. *Homosexual Behavior Among Males.* Englewood Cliffs, NJ: Prentice Hall, 1971.

Crompton, L. *Homosexuality and the Sickness Theory.* San Francisco: Society for Individual Rights, 1963.

DeMartino, M. F., ed. *Sexual Behavior and Personality Characteristics.* New York: Grove Press, 1966.

Ellis, A. *Homosexuality: Its Causes and Cure.* Secaucus, NJ: Lyle Stuart, 1965.

Freedman & Kaplan, eds. *Comprehensive Textbook of Psychiatry.* Baltimore: Williams & Wilkins Co., 1967.

Ford, C. & Beach, F. *Patterns of Sexual Behavior*. New York: Ace Books, 1951.

Goldenson, *Encyclopedia of Human Behavior*. Garden City, NY: Doubleday & Co., 1920.

Hatterer, L. J. *Changing Homosexuality in the Male*. New York: McGraw-Hill Book Co., 1970.

Henry, G. W. *Sex Variants*. New York: Harper, 1941.

Hirschfield, M. *Sexual Anomolies*. New York: Emerson Books, 1956.

Kahn, S. *Mentality and Homosexuality*. Boston: Meador Publications, 1937.

Lief, H. I. *Medical Aspects of Human Sexuality*. Baltimore: Williams & Wilkins, 1975.

Maccoby, E., ed. *The Development of Sex Differences*. Stanford, CA: Stanford University Press, 1966.

Marmor, J., ed. *Sexual Inversion: The Multiple Roots of Homosexuality*. New York: Basic Books, 1965.

Moll, A. *Perversions of the Sexual Instinct*. New York: Julian Press, 1931.

Money, J. *Sex Errors of the Body*. Baltimore, MD: Johns Hopkins Press, 1968.

Money, J., ed. *Sex Research: New Developments*. New York: Holt, Rinehart & Winston, 1965.

Ovesey, L. *Homosexuality and Pseudohomosexuality*. New York: Science House, 1969.

Rosen, I., ed. *The Pathology and Treatment of Sexual Deviation*. New York: Oxford University Press, 1964.

Ruitenbeek, H., ed. *Psychotherapy of Perversions*. Secaucus, NJ: Citadel Press, 1967.

Socarides, C. W. *The Overt Homosexual*. New York: Grune & Stratton, 1968.

Stekel, W. *The Homosexual Neurosis*. Boston: R. G. Badger, 1953.

————. *Sexual Aberrations*. New York: Grove Press, 1964.

Walker, K. *The Physiology of Sex*. Oxford: Penguin Books, 1954.

Winokur, G., ed. *Determinants of Human Sexual Behavior*. Springfield, IL: C. C Thomas, 1963.

Bibliography of Articles on Homosexuality, Mainly in Religious Periodicals (1949-early 1977)

America, Jan. 25, 1958:485–486.
　　　　　June 3, 1967:802–803.
　　　　　Nov. 14, 1970:406.
　　　　　Feb. 6, 1971:113.
　　　　　Sept. 14, 1974:117.
American Ecclesiastical Review, Feb. 1968:122–129.
　　　　　　　　　　　　　　Jan. 1971:42.
　　　　　　　　　　　　　　Nov. 1973:602.
American Opinion, Nov. 1971:39.
Asbury Seminarian, 25:6–9.
Awake, Jan. 8, 1964:14–16.
Banner, Nov. 8, 1968:4.
　　　　　Aug. 28, 1970:8.
Bulletin of the National Guild of Catholic Psychiatrists Dec. 1972.
Catholic Lawyer, 9:4–10, 94–105.
　　　　　　　　10:90–108.
Catholic World, June 1971:121.
　　　　　　　　July 1971:183.
Change, Oct. 1971:38.
Chelsea Journal, March–April 1976:65.
Christian Advocate, Sept. 13, 1973:7.
Christian Century, 81:1581.
　　　　　　　　84:1587.
　　　　　　　　85:744–745.
　　　　　　　　88:(March 3, 1971):275,281.

(Dec. 15, 1971):1468.
89:660–661, 713–716.
91:591–593.
92:243–244, 474–475.

Christian Life, 29:(Oct. 1967):38–39.
37:(June 1975):24–25.
38:(June 1976):20–21.

Christian Ministry, Jan. 1972:44.

Christian Reformed, Church Report 42 of *Acts of Synod* (1973).

Christian Standard, July 13, 1975:8.

Christianity and Crisis, 23:175–9, 204–206.
24:223.
26:84–85, 135.
27:270–271, 314.
33:63–68.
34:147–149, 178–181.
37, no. 5:63–67.
37, nos. 9–10.

Christianity Today, 10:(Mar. 4, 1966):51–52.
12:(Jan. 19, 1968):24.
(Feb. 16, 1968):29–30.
(Mar. 1, 1968):23.
13:(July 18, 1969):7–10.
14:(Mar. 13, 1970):31–32.
(Sept. 11, 1970):48–50.
15:(Dec. 4, 1970):40–41.
16:(June 23, 1972):27–28.
17:(Sept. 28, 1973):8–12.
(Feb. 16, 1973):12–18.
18:(Apr. 26, 1974):13–14.
(Sept. 27, 1974):11–14.
19:(Jan. 31, 1975):28–30.
(Mar. 28, 1975):38–39.
(July 4, 1975):23–24.
(Sept. 12, 1975):14–17.
20:(Mar. 12, 1976):53–55.
21:(Feb. 4, 1977):55–56.
(Mar. 4, 1977):2–5.
(July 8, 1977):8–10, 36.
(July 29, 1977):38.

Church and Society, 67, no. 5: (May–June, 1977).

Church Herald, Jan. 12, 1968:10.
Jan. 19, 1968:14.
June 27, 1975:6.

Clergy Review, Aug. 1963.

Commonweal, Apr. 6, 1973:103, 107.
        May 24, 1974:275–276.
        May 31, 1974:304.
        Feb. 15, 1974:479.

Concern, June 15, 1963.
        Apr. 15, 1966:10, 11.

Continuum, Summer 1967.

Cross Currents, Spring 1970:221.

Dignity: A Monthly Newsletter for Catholic Homophiles and Concerned Heterophiles, (755 Boylston Street, Room 413, Boston, Mass. 02116).

Dublin Review, Summer 1965.
        Summer 1967.

Engage/Social Action, 1:21–24.
        3:28–31, 32–33, 36–37, 53–54.
        4:6–11.

Episcopalian, June 1971:17.

Eternity, 13:(Oct. 1962):22–25.
        (Feb. 1970):8.
        23:(Aug. 1972):23–25.

Expository Times, 78:356–360.

Good News Broadcaster, March 1974:4.

Herald of Holiness, Nov. 7, 1973:17.

His, 26:(Feb. 1966):14–18.
        (Mar. 1966):5–9.
        31:(Jan. 1971):24–25.
        34:(March 1974):20–21.

Homiletic and Pastoral Review, Dec. 1957.
        Sept. 1966.
        May 1968.
        July–Sept. 1970.

Homophile Studies: One Institute Quarterly, (2256 Venice Blvd., Los Angeles, CA 90006).

Integrity: Gay Episcopal Forum, (701 Orange Street, No. 6, Fort Valley, GA 31030).

International Journal of Religious Education, Nov.–Dec. 1971:14.

Journal for the Scientific Study of Religion, 13:479–481.

Jurist, 20:441–459.
        21:394–422.

Journal of American Scientific Affiliation, 16:(Dec. 1964):112–114.
        29:(Sept. 1977):103–110.

Journal of Homosexuality, (53 W. 72nd St., New York, NY 10023).

Journal of Marriage and Family, May 1966:155.

Journal of the New York Mission of the Metropolitan Community Church, (201 West 13th Street, New York, NY).

Journal of Pastoral Practice, 1, no. 2.

Journal of Psychology and Theology, 2:(Summer 1974):163–173.
3:94–98.

Journal of Religion and Health, 6:17–32, 217–234.
7:61–78, 368–370.

Journal for the Scientific Study of Religion, 13:479–481.

Jurist, 20:441–459. 21:394–422.

Ladder, The, (P.O. Box 5025, Washington Station, Reno, NV 89503).

Liberation, (Sanctuary House, Arlington, VA).

Liquorian, 54:18–24.

Living Church, Jan. 8, 1967.

Logos, 6:(May 1976):10–13.

Marriage, 53:(1971):38–43.

Moody Monthly, 74:(Sept. 1973):35–37.
75:(Sept. 1974):82–87.
76:(Nov. 1975):23.

Motive, Mar.–Apr. 1969:61.

National Catholic Reporter, 9, no. 38.

Pastoral Psychology, 6:31–42, 43–45, 44–53.
9:46–49.
13:35–42.
21:29–37.
22:41–44, 45–46.
23:50–58.

Pentecostal Evangel, Feb. 21, 1971:18.
Feb. 29, 1976:4.

Presbyterian Church in America, Resolutions of Fifth General Assembly (1977).

Presbyterian Guardian, 46, nos. 5–6:4–5, 6–8.

Presbyterian Journal, June 26, 1974:12.
Oct. 15, 1975:12.
Dec. 17, 1975:10.
Nov. 30, 1977.

Psychology Today, Mar. 1975:28.

Radical Religion, 1:19–21.

Religion in Life, 43:(Winter 1974):436–444.
Winter 1966:760.

Review and Expositor, 68:217–226.

Review for Religions, 27:(Sept. 1968):880–882.

Social Action, 34:5–47.

Social Compass, 21, no. 3:355–360.

Social Progress, 58:5–47.

Spectrum, 47:14–17.

Studia Theologica, 28, no. 2:111–152.

St. Joseph Magazine, Jan.–May 1965.

Tablet, 202:(Dec. 1957):272–278.

Theological Studies, 16:86–108.
                   33:100–119.

Theology, 55:47–52.
          58:459–463.

Thomist, 35:(1971):447–481.

Trends, July–Aug. 1973 (UPCUSA publication).

Union Seminary Quarterly Review, 25:439–455.

United Church Herald, July–Aug. 1972:35.

United Evangelical Action, 36:(Winter 1977):14.

U.S. Catholic, Oct. 1967:12.
              Sept. 1972:6.
              Aug. 1975:6.

War Cry, March 4, 1972:2.

World Student Christian Federation Books, 3, no. 2:16–23.

Scripture Index